Cambridge Elements ≡

Elements in Criminology
edited by
David Weisburd
George Mason University, Virginia
Hebrew University of Jerusalem

CONFRONTING SCHOOL VIOLENCE

A Synthesis of Six Decades of Research

Jillian J. Turanovic
Florida State University

Travis C. Pratt
University of Cincinnati

Teresa C. Kulig
University of Nebraska at Omaha

Francis T. Cullen
University of Cincinnati

CAMBRIDGE
UNIVERSITY PRESS

CAMBRIDGE
UNIVERSITY PRESS

University Printing House, Cambridge CB2 8BS, United Kingdom

One Liberty Plaza, 20th Floor, New York, NY 10006, USA

477 Williamstown Road, Port Melbourne, VIC 3207, Australia

314–321, 3rd Floor, Plot 3, Splendor Forum, Jasola District Centre,
New Delhi – 110025, India

103 Penang Road, #05–06/07, Visioncrest Commercial, Singapore 238467

Cambridge University Press is part of the University of Cambridge.

It furthers the University's mission by disseminating knowledge in the pursuit of
education, learning, and research at the highest international levels of excellence.

www.cambridge.org
Information on this title: www.cambridge.org/9781108799850
DOI: 10.1017/9781108891998

© Jillian J. Turanovic, Travis C. Pratt, Teresa C. Kulig, and Francis T. Cullen 2022

First published 2022

A catalogue record for this publication is available from the British Library.

ISBN 978-1-108-79985-0 Paperback
ISSN 2633-3341 (online)
ISSN 2633-3333 (print)

Confronting School Violence

A Synthesis of Six Decades of Research

Elements in Criminology

DOI: 10.1017/9781108891998
First published online: February 2022

Jillian J. Turanovic
Florida State University

Travis C. Pratt
University of Cincinnati

Teresa C. Kulig
University of Nebraska at Omaha

Francis T. Cullen
University of Cincinnati

Author for correspondence: Jillian J. Turanovic, jturanovic@fsu.edu

Abstract: School violence is a significant social concern. To better understand its sources, a comprehensive meta-analysis of the school violence and victimization literature was undertaken. Across 761 studies, the relative effects of 30 different individual-, school-, and community-level correlates were assessed (8,790 effect size estimates). Violence and victimization were conceptualized broadly to include various forms of aggression and crime at school. The results revealed that the strongest correlates of school violence perpetration were antisocial behavior, deviant peers, antisocial attitudes, victimization, and peer rejection; and that the strongest correlates of school victimization were prior/other victimization, social competence, risk avoidance, antisocial behavior, and peer rejection. Extracurricular activities and school security devices had among the weakest associations in the meta-analysis, and several traditional criminological predictors did not perform well in the school context. We conclude with recommendations for theory, future research, and policy.

Keywords: bullying, meta-analysis, school violence, victimization

ISBNs: 9781108799850 (PB), 9781108891998 (OC)
ISSNs: 2633-3341 (online), 2633-3333 (print)

Contents

1 Introduction

Schools are supposed to be safe places for children. The problem, however, is that their safety is often compromised in ways that seem to have gotten worse over the last several decades. High-profile incidents of lethal violence in American schools, for example, are not in short supply. Indeed, mass school shootings have established names like Columbine High School, Sandy Hook Elementary School, and Marjory Stoneman Douglas High School as permanent parts of the American violence landscape (Cullen, 2009; Fridel, 2021; Jonson, 2017). And as tragic as these events were, they represent only a portion of the several hundred deadly shootings that have occurred in schools in the United States since 1970 (CHDS K-12 School Shooting Database, 2020).

Still, school shootings are just one part of a much broader problem of school violence in general (Finkelhor et al., 2016; Myers et al., 2020; Rose, 2018). Stacked upon the fear of lethal violence that students have to contend with are the more frequent occurrences of school-based bullying, harassment, aggression, and intimidation faced on a daily basis (Chouhy et al., 2017; Fisher et al., 2017; Kelly & McBride, 2020). Recent national estimates reveal that over 800,000 instances of victimization at school (including theft and nonfatal violent victimization) occur each year among students aged 12–18 years (Wang et al., 2020). The simple truth, then, is that victimization in school affects a lot of kids.

This fact is critically important since school victimization – just like victimization that occurs in other situational and social contexts – has been linked to a wide array of problematic outcomes in both the short- and long-term (Polanin et al., 2021). Research has shown that youths who are victimized at school have a greater likelihood of experiencing a variety of mental health problems, such as anxiety, depression, and suicidal ideation (Duru & Balkis, 2018; Hatchel et al., 2019; Hinduja & Patchin, 2019), and increased risks of behavioral problems, such as engaging in substance abuse and other forms of delinquency (Connell et al., 2017; Deryol & Wilcox, 2020; Sullivan et al., 2006). Research also reveals that victimized students tend to have weakened school attachments and demonstrate poorer levels of academic performance (Fite et al., 2014; Randa et al., 2019), that they are more likely to be rejected by their peers (Faris & Felmlee, 2014; Turanovic & Young, 2016; Zimmer-Gembeck, 2016), and that they score lower on general indicators of well-being (Varela et al., 2019). These consequences may extend well into the life course, as victimization during childhood and adolescence has been linked to a range of social, health, and emotional problems in adulthood, including criminal offending (Arseneault et al., 2010; Turanovic & Pratt, 2015; Wright et al., 2019).

It is this wide array of negative consequences that has raised the public profile of school violence in recent years and solidified it as a significant social problem (Forster et al., 2020). As a result, there is arguably more political pressure now to "do something" about the problem of school violence than there ever has been before (Lee et al., 2020). And in response, dozens of new school-based violence interventions have been developed and implemented, ranging from antibullying educational campaigns, to the development of "threat assessment" models for at-risk students (Borum et al., 2010; Cornell, 2020; Jiménez-Barbero et al., 2020), to legislation that criminalizes bullying behavior (Brank et al., 2012; Cosgrove & Nickerson, 2017; Hatzenbuehler et al., 2017). Schools around the United States have also placed police officers on site (Counts et al., 2018), implemented a host of "get-tough" policies for violent behavior (Collier et al., 2019; Gottfredson, 2017), adopted a wide range of security measures for reducing potential opportunities for violence (e.g., cameras, metal detectors, transparent backpacks; Tanner-Smith et al., 2018), and even developed policies and practices intended to reduce the death toll should extreme violence occur (e.g., lock down and active shooter drills; Jonson et al., 2020; Schildkraut & Nickerson, 2020).

But successfully addressing a problem like school violence – just like trying to solve any other problem for that matter – assumes that we have a good understanding of what influences the problem in the first place. Yet we do not currently have a firm handle on which factors are most strongly associated with school violence and victimization that might be targeted for interventions (Bushman et al., 2016). And the absence of such knowledge is not the result of the absence of research – there are hundreds of studies on school violence, conducted by scholars working in a variety of academic disciplines (including criminology, sociology, education, social work, public health, and psychology), dating back over the last six decades (Benbenishty et al., 2005; Brank et al., 2012; Olweus, 2013). Instead, what is holding us back is the relative dearth of efforts to systematically organize what these studies collectively tell us about the nature and sources of violence at school. Without such an effort, we are left with a disjointed way of thinking about the problem, with different explanations of school violence and victimization spread across several academic fields, and with such scholarly work rarely crossing disciplinary boundaries. This lack of consensus is consequential because how we think about the sources of a problem inevitably has implications for how we think about its potential solution.

In this context, the current project attempts to discern what the existing literature – contributed over the past six decades – tells us about the sources of school violence and victimization by undertaking a comprehensive meta-analysis of research studies. In what follows, we review how scholars from diverse academic fields have approached the investigation of school violence and victimization theoretically and empirically. Building on this thinking and the large body of research it has yielded, we then explain the research strategy informing the current project. Following that, we describe the results of the meta-analysis, and then discuss the implications for theory, research, and policy.

1.1 Thinking about School Violence

No academic discipline "owns" the study of violence. To be sure, violent behavior and its consequences have been studied by scholars in many fields – ranging from sociology to psychology (Laub, 2004; West & Farrington, 1973), from political science to economics (Donohue & Levitt, 2001; Wilson & Herrnstein, 1985), to myriad others in between (Jeffrey, 1978; Walsh & Ellis, 2007) – and all of them have something important to say about why such behavior occurs. Yet it is criminology, an admittedly interdisciplinary field, that is fully devoted to problems like identifying the sources and consequences of criminal violence. As a result, there is a substantively useful demarcation to explore with respect to how scholars think about the nature of school violence and victimization across disciplines, specifically with respect to the major theoretical perspectives that are often used. And it may come as a bit of a surprise that there is not always overlap between them.

For example, traditional criminological perspectives have a long history of being applied to violent behavior generally. Early sociological models saw violence through the lens of community dynamics that facilitated juvenile delinquency (e.g., a breakdown in sources of social control and the transmission of attitudes supportive of crime and violence; Shaw & McKay, 1942), through peer interactions and the competition of criminal and noncriminal value systems (Sutherland, 1924), and through the strains induced by the American brand of coupling economic stratification with the cultural goal of achieving economic success (Merton, 1938; see also Cloward & Ohlin, 1960; Cohen, 1955). These explanations were largely replaced in the 1960s with those that focused on how criminal behavior – including violent behavior – is learned through a process of modeling and reinforcement (Burgess & Akers, 1966), as well as how such behavior could be the product of weakened social bonds to prosocial people and institutions (Hirschi, 1969). More contemporary perspectives have revived the rational choice tradition – the idea that crime and violence happen because people are not sufficiently afraid of punishment (see Becker, 1968; Gibbs, 1975) – and others that have emphasized the importance of individuals' levels of self-control (Gottfredson & Hirschi, 1990).[1]

All of these ideas have influenced mainstream criminological research on the sources of school violence (Gottfredson, 2001). In this way, it is common within criminology to approach the study of "street crime" and "school crime" in similar ways – where school violence and bullying are viewed, to some extent, as "a microcosm of offending in the community" (Farrington, 1993, p. 383). Scholars have, for instance, assessed the relationships between offending at school and measures of school and community context (e.g., indicators of economic deprivation, community crime rates, and violent school context; see Baker, 1998; Wilcox, Augustine et al., 2006; Wilcox Rountree, 2000), deviant peer associations and antisocial attitudes (Ousey & Wilcox, 2005; Pratt et al., 2010), various forms of emotional affect and strain (James et al., 2015; Lee & Cohen, 2008), bonds to school and to parents (Georgiou, 2009; Peguero & Jiang, 2014; Savage, 2014), and levels of self-control (Chui & Chan, 2015; Moon & Alarid, 2015). And the results of this work largely mirror those associated with offending in general – that support is found for each of these sets of variables, at least under some circumstances, but that much of the variation in offending at school is left unexplained.

Other disciplines – from education, to developmental and school psychology – tend to draw more heavily from social and developmental perspectives that center on status enhancement (Aizpitarte et al., 2019; Dahlberg & Potter, 2001; Herrenkohl et al., 2000) and social adjustment (Crick & Dodge, 1994; Dodge et al., 2008; Estévez et al., 2009). Peer relationships are a fundamental part of the lives of school-aged children, and a core component of those relationships is the status hierarchy that youths inevitably have to navigate (Destin et al., 2012; Fournier, 2009; Juvonen & Graham, 2001). In the 1950s, psychology research emerged linking various forms of aggression to status and popularity within peer groups. Some of this early work found that certain forms of aggression among schoolboys – such as provoked aggression versus unprovoked outbursts – were met with approval by peers (Lesser, 1959). Seminal research on school bullying by Olewus (1978) also found that boys who bullied

---

[1] Other criminological perspectives, of course, exist that attempt to explain violent behavior. These range from conflict/Marxian and relative deprivation theories (Blau & Blau, 1982; Chambliss & Seidman, 1971), to feminist and critical perspectives (Renzetti, 2013; Young, 1999), to integrated perspectives that attempt to draw various ideas together under a common framework (Braithwaite, 1989; Colvin, 2000; Unnever & Gabbidon, 2011). Nevertheless, perspectives like social disorganization, differential association/social learning, strain, rational choice/deterrence, and social (and self-) control have arguably formed the "core" of criminology for nearly a century (Cullen et al., 2006).

other students were relatively popular and often had the support of two or three other boys in the classroom.

A large literature in developmental psychology has since developed that considers factors such as popularity, social preference, and peer acceptance in relation to school aggression (de Bruyn et al., 2010; Olweus, 1977; Postigo et al., 2012; Pouwels et al., 2018). Victimizing others – whether through aggression, bullying, or outright violence – is perceived by some youths as a viable strategy for establishing themselves higher up on the social ladder (Faris et al., 2020; Forsberg & Thornberg, 2016; Lantos & Halpern, 2015; Salmivalli, 2010). School aggression is therefore considered within some developmental frameworks to be a strategic, instrumental behavior that enables youths to gain and maintain a dominant social position (Faris & Felmlee, 2011; Hawley, 1999; Rodkin et al., 2006). This view is in contrast to some mainstream criminological perspectives that explain aggression primarily as the product of impulsivity, poor emotion regulation, or peer rejection (Garofalo & Velotti, 2017; Gottfredson & Hirschi, 1990; Hirschi, 1969). Indeed, psychological and developmental research on bullying suggests that bullies are calculating in their aggression and that they "score high when asked how important it is to be visible, influential, and admired" (Juvonen & Graham, 2014, p. 164). Consequently, much of this work focuses on how social and interpersonal skills (like social competence) can help youths mitigate the negative aspects of social relationships and peer rejection, and cope with the stressors associated with surviving the social hierarchy minefield in nonviolent ways (Arsenio & Lemerise, 2001; Camodeca et al., 2015).

Of course, disciplinary boundaries are not impermeable, and perspectives on developmental criminology have proliferated over the past several decades as well, integrating explanations from psychology (Farrington et al., 2018; Loeber & Le Blanc, 1990; Tremblay & Craig, 1995). And there are some factors – such as childhood trauma and victimization – that are central to the study of school violence across multiple fields (DeCamp & Newby, 2015; Forster et al., 2020; Olweus, 1978). A large body of interdisciplinary scholarship also emphasizes ecological factors (Bronfenbrenner, 1979), such as school climate, that shape the norms, values, rules, and structure of a school (Espelage & Swearer, 2004; Gage et al., 2014; Steffgen et al., 2013). Schools with a positive climate are typically those where students feel safe (emotionally and physically), and where collaboration, respect, and positive social relationships exist among students and teachers (National School Climate Council, 2007). A positive school climate is thought to improve status struggles – and, by extension, the perpetration of bullying, aggression, and violence – by improving peer support, lessening peer rejection, and fostering caring and supportive peer relationships (Espelage et al., 2014).

But, broadly speaking, just like with the study of aggression and violence in general, different disciplines tend to favor their own theoretical perspectives (Dooley, 2021) – and by extension, different sets of predictors – when it comes to the study of school violence. Within criminology, the focus is often placed on traditional correlates, such as self-control, social bond, strain, social learning, social disorganization, and rational choice constructs (Moon & Alarid, 2015; Ousey & Wilcox, 2005; Unnever & Cornell, 2003; Walters, 2018; Wilcox & Clayton, 2001). In other fields, the focus is more commonly placed on social-interactional and parenting skills (Patterson, 1986), social information processing (Dodge & Coie, 1987), social dominance (Sidanius & Pratto, 1999), social cognition (Swearer et al., 2014), social exclusion anxiety (Schott & Søndergaard, 2014), and diathesis–stress (Swearer & Hymel, 2015). So, while interdisciplinary scholarship certainly exists, there is a tendency for research on school violence to be produced within academic disciplines that is siloed from the others. Synthesizing this work – and assessing it as a whole – is critical to transcend disciplinary boundaries, and to determine what are the most important correlates of school violence.

1.2 Thinking about School Victimization

Similar to the study of violence, the study of victimization is markedly inter-disciplinary. Research on childhood victimization in particular has origins in medicine, social work, and psychology (Kempe et al., 1962; Olweus, 1978; Zalba, 1966), and is today one of the most widely studied phenomena within the social sciences (Finkelhor, 2008; Hymel & Swearer, 2015; Metzler et al., 2017). There is no shortage of perspectives that have attempted to identify the complex sources of bullying, harassment, and violent victimization that can significantly impact the lives of youths. But, just like with the study of violence, there are differences between the main theoretical perspectives used to explain victim-ization within the field of criminology versus other academic disciplines.

Within criminology, for example, opportunity perspectives are favored (Wilcox & Cullen, 2018). And, for the past several decades, lifestyle (Hindelang et al., 1978) and routine activity (Cohen & Felson, 1979) theories have dominated the study of victimization. Although these two perspectives differ in their emphasis on risky behaviors (Pratt & Turanovic, 2016), they are similar in that they both view victimization in terms of the convergence in time and space of a motivated offender, a suitable target/victim, and the absence of capable guardianship. Specifically, Hindelang and colleagues (1978) observed that people who share certain demographic characteristics (e.g., age, sex, or race) are either more or less likely to be victimized. These differences in victimization risk were viewed as a function of the lifestyles that different demographic groups engaged in. Individuals who engaged in lifestyles that were *risky* – those that routinely exposed them to "high risk times, places, and people" – were more likely to experience victimization (Hindelang et al., 1978, p. 245). These lifestyle patterns were also viewed as being shaped by "structural constraints," or social forces stemming from inequalities in the social structure, such as economic deprivation and racial segregation (South & Deane, 1993).

On the other hand, Cohen and Felson's (1979) routine activity theory emphasized that people do not need to be doing risky things to be victimized. Routine activity theory was instead used to explain how victimization could still occur even in the absence of traditional criminogenic social conditions such as poverty (Felson & Cohen, 1980). Crime and victimization were seen as rooted in the routines of "everyday life" that put people in the presence of others, such as leaving the home and going to work (Felson & Boba, 2010) – the sorts of daily activities that "separate many people from those they trust and the property they value" (Cohen & Felson, 1979, p. 591).

In recent years, lifestyle and routine activity theories have been extended in a few key ways. For instance, risky lifestyle and self-control theories have been coupled together in an integrated perspective on victimization (Pratt et al., 2014; Turanovic & Pratt, 2014; Turanovic et al., 2015). This perspective recognizes that individuals with poor self-control are more likely to engage in risky behaviors that bring them into proximity to dangerous places and people (e.g., partying late at night or engaging in criminal activities) where the opportunity for victimization is high (Schreck, 1999). Additionally, routine activity theory – which was originally put forth as a macro-level explanation of changes in crime rate trends – has been further extended to individuals. An expansive array of routine activities has been linked to victimization, including unstructured socializing with friends, going to the library, and hanging out in public spaces, such as in gardens, cafés, coffee shops, and stores (Bunch et al., 2014; Felson et al., 2013; Tanner et al., 2015).

So, when it comes to victimization at school, for the most part, criminological research tends to approach the problem in the same way as the study of victimization more generally: from the opportunity perspectives of lifestyle and routine activity theories. As such, much of the school victimization research produced in mainstream criminology focuses heavily on students' behavioral routines. These include behaviors that are risky (e.g., consuming drugs and alcohol, engaging in various antisocial behavior, or hanging out with delinquent peers) – especially when they occur in high-risk contexts (e.g., in schools characterized by a culture of violence, or in schools located in disadvantaged and violent communities) – which seem to be important predictors of school victimization, at least some of the time (Astor et al., 2002; Khanhkham et al., 2020; Zaykowski & Gunter, 2012). Criminological research has also focused on behaviors that are more mundane, such as participating in extracurricular activities (e.g., sports, spirit groups, and academic clubs), which seem to generate more inconsistent findings (Cecen-Celik & Keith, 2019; Popp & Peguero, 2011). Some research has also revealed that youths' levels of self-control can influence their risks of victimization at school, net of their risky behaviors (Deryol et al., 2017; Kulig et al., 2019; Tillyer et al., 2018; Wilcox et al., 2009). But, these findings, too, are mixed. Some studies suggest that low self-control – the relevance of which hinges on the assumption that youths have autonomy to choose what they want to do and when or where they want to do it – is not a strong or consistent predictor of victimization at school, which is a relatively structured environment (Kulig et al., 2017; Unnever & Cornell, 2003). It therefore seems that traditional criminological perspectives, when applied to the study of victimization at school, are leaving some significant gaps unfilled.

Some of those gaps might be addressed by perspectives that are more central within other disciplines. In fields such as education and developmental psychology, the problem of victimization at school is often seen as less of the product of risky or unstructured activities and more of the product of "vulnerability" that stems from deviating from group norms (Blake et al., 2016; Eisenberg et al., 2016; Juvonen & Graham, 2001). Personal characteristics or attributes that are outside of a child's control can thus contribute to the risk of victimization (Finkelhor & Asdigian, 1996; Olweus, 1978). For example, children with physical or cognitive disabilities (Christensen et al., 2012; Son et al., 2012) and LGBT youths (lesbian, gay, bisexual, and transgender) are at higher risk of being bullied and victimized at school (Myers et al., 2020). Any nonnormative characteristics that make youths stand out from their peers – whether it be related to their race or ethnicity, appearance, or identity – place them at risk of being shunned, stigmatized, or viewed as a "social misfit" (Wright et al., 1986). Children who occupy a marginal social status are at risk for victimization because they are unlikely to be supported or defended by peer group members (Juvonen & Graham, 2014; Troop-Gordon, 2017).

These "in-group" versus "out-group" dynamics are also viewed as being shaped by various school-level factors (Thomas et al., 2018). Victimization is more common in schools and classrooms characterized by peer norms that support bullying and aggression, peer conflict, and where there is an imbalance of power that is tipped in favor of a few students (Garandeau et al., 2014; Hymel

& Swearer, 2015). Alternatively, in schools with increased social capital and a positive school climate – such as where there are clear rules that govern student conduct, there are more equitable peer dynamics, and teachers have more disapproving views toward aggression and bullying – students tend to have lower risks of victimization (Saarento et al., 2013). Of course, just as with the study of violent behavior and offending at school, there is interdisciplinary overlap between criminological research and scholarship produced in other fields (Beelmann & Lösel, 2021; Gottfredson & DiPietro, 2011). However, the predominant perspectives that are used within criminology to study victimization at school tend to be somewhat unique from other disciplines (Deryol et al., 2017; Wilcox et al., 2009).

1.3 The Current Project

These considerations make it clear that school violence is a multifaceted problem. Drawing from different theoretical perspectives, across a wide range of disciplines, scholars have identified a lengthy roster of characteristics – at the individual, school, and community levels – that can potentially influence violence and victimization at school (Thomas et al., 2018). At the individual level, these have included student demographic characteristics (e.g., age, sex, race, socioeconomic status), traditional criminological risk factors (e.g., self-control, deviant peers, antisocial attitudes, substance use) and protective factors (e.g., bonds to parents, bonds to school), school activities and indicators of school success (e.g., extracurricular activities, school avoidance, academic achievement), factors related to peer relationships and social dynamics (e.g., peer rejection, popularity, social competence), and markers of vulnerability, such as LGBT identification, or having a physical or learning disability. At the school level, the focus has been placed on school climate, school disorder, school size, urbanicity, and the use of visible school security devices (like metal detectors and cameras). Even characteristics of the communities in which schools are embedded have been examined, where factors such as economic deprivation, community crime, and community disorder have been linked to school violence and victimization.

With so many factors being examined across different academic disciplines, it is difficult to determine what are the most important correlates of school violence. Evidently, there are a number of individual, institutional, and community factors that all seem to play at least some role in explaining why some youths are more at risk to either engage in violence or to be victimized at school. But because of this embarrassment of riches – so many studies from so many diverse sources – we really do not have a clear picture as to which factors are more important than others, which factors have general effects (versus those that make a difference for particular forms of violence and not for others), or which factors make the best candidates to target for change with policy interventions. What is needed now is a systematic effort to take stock of this literature – to organize it in a way that would be most useful for guiding future research and informing interventions to combat violence in schools. The purpose of this Element is to accomplish that very task.

Accordingly, we present the results of a comprehensive meta-analysis of the quantitative literature on school violence that has been produced over the past six decades. We identify the relative impacts of various individual, school, and community factors in order to determine the strongest (and weakest) correlates of school violence and victimization. Although several reviews and smaller meta-analyses of this literature have been undertaken – including those that focus on a specific set of risk factors, or on a specific outcome, such as bullying – there have not yet been efforts to make sense of the broader spectrum of research produced on the sources of school violence in the form of a large-scale meta-analysis.

The Element proceeds as follows. In Section 2, we present an overview of the methods used in our study. Meta-analytic methods are described in terms of their key advantages, and we detail the processes used to generate our sample of 8,790 effect size estimates that are drawn from 761 studies – making it one of the largest meta-analyses to ever be conducted in the social sciences. We also describe in this section the full roster of thirty different individual, school, and community correlates of school violence and victimization that we assess, as well as the statistical strategies that we employ to estimate their relative effects. Given that problems of school violence fall on the same spectrum as other harmful behaviors – ranging from bullying, to delinquency, to bringing weapons to school – we conceptualize the perpetration and victimization of school violence broadly to also include various forms of interpersonal aggression and delinquency at school.

The results of our analyses are presented in two sections – one for the perpetration of school violence, aggression, and delinquency (Section 3), and another for victimization at school (Section 4). There is a well-documented relationship between offending and victimization, where offenders and victims often seem to be drawn from the same pool of people (Gottfredson, 1981). This pattern is so consistent empirically that the "victim–offender overlap" is one of the most well-known findings in the criminological literature (Berg & Mulford, 2020; Lauritsen & Laub, 2007). Even so, the act of inflicting harm on others – particularly when it comes to violence – is not the same thing as being on the receiving end of it. Thus, analyzing perpetration and victimization at school separately will allow us to consider a number of important research questions, including: (1) What are the factors that end up being strongly related to school violence perpetration *and* victimization? (2) What are the factors that end up being weakly related to both outcomes? (3) And which factors appear to be uniquely linked to just perpetration *or* victimization? The answers to these questions can help us identify those factors that should be targeted in interventions for school safety generally (i.e., interventions intended to reduce perpetration *and* victimization), those factors that should probably be ignored, and those factors that should be included in more tailored interventions specific to perpetration or to victimization. Finally, in Section 5, we discuss our results in terms of their key implications for theory, research, and policy regarding school violence. In the end, our broader purpose is to provide a clear picture of how we can confront the problem of school violence in a fair, equitable, and evidence-based way.

2 Methodology

In this section, we describe the methods that we use to meta-analyze the literature on school violence. A meta-analysis – or "quantitative synthesis" – entails "the application of statistical procedures to collections of empirical findings for the purpose of integrating, synthesizing, and making sense of them" (Niemi, 1986, p. 5). This method allows for the calculation of precise estimates of the "effect size" of certain relationships so that more concrete inferences can be made about their relative importance. Conducting a meta-analysis is especially useful when a body of literature is large, and when a consensus has yet to be reached concerning the relative importance of correlates of an outcome of interest (Pratt, 2010) – two properties that certainly characterize the literature on violence in school.

2.1 The Importance of Meta-Analysis

A key strength of a meta-analysis is that it can provide a single estimate of the magnitude, or effect size, of a specified relationship between two variables across multiple research studies (Siddaway et al., 2019). A meta-analysis can therefore determine which factors at the individual, school, and community levels are strong, moderate, weak, or null correlates of school violence and victimization.

Another benefit of a meta-analysis is that it can provide useful information about how effect sizes vary across a body of literature (Turanovic & Pratt, 2021). In the present case, a meta-analysis can allow us to see whether the strength of a particular risk factor, such as deviant peer associations, is stronger or weaker for particular forms of violence, aggression, or delinquency at school (e.g., bullying others versus engaging in violent offending). This knowledge could provide insight regarding the potential need (or not) for behavior-specific policy or program interventions. As such, a meta-analysis can also show which factors seem to be "general" correlates of various forms of school violence, aggression, delinquency, and victimization. This information would indicate that any policy or program being developed to address violence in school would need to keep those factors in mind. This is what meta-analysis can do – and it is critically needed at this point in the literature to illustrate what kinds of policy interventions are likely to be most effective, and where to go next with respect to studying school violence.

2.2 Criteria for Inclusion and Exclusion of Studies

To provide a comprehensive assessment of the literature, our inclusion criteria were set broadly: all published peer-reviewed studies printed in English that presented a statistical relationship between any of our identified individual, school, or community predictor domains, and any form of school violence perpetration or victimization against students were eligible for inclusion in the meta-analysis. Such studies included various forms of school bullying, aggression, and delinquency. Studies that did not specify whether perpetration or victimization occurred specifically while at school or on school grounds were excluded, as were studies of victimization and perpetration that took place online, against teachers, or that assessed school violence perpetration or victimization at the aggregate level only (i.e., at the school level). Thus, the meta-analysis includes only studies that assessed school violence at the individual level. We focused exclusively on students in primary and secondary schools (kindergarten through twelfth grade). Studies that were based on preschoolers or post-secondary students were not included.

2.3 Sample

Quantitative studies published up to January 2019 were gathered in three phases. First, exhaustive electronic searches were conducted through seven different online databases: Google Scholar, EBSCO, Wiley, Sage, Taylor & Francis, Springer, and Science Direct. We conducted our searches using key terms "school," "student," and "peer," which we linked with "violen*," "victim*," "bully*," "aggress*," "attack," "shoot*," "harm," "crim*," "offend*," "delinquen*," "threat*," "fight*," "hit," "steal," "intimidat*," "safety," and "weapon." Second, we searched through the electronic holdings of 106 academic journals across different research fields that are known to publish on school violence and victimization (see Appendix A for a list of these journals). Third, the reference lists of previously published narrative reviews and meta-analyses were examined for any remaining studies that were not located in prior searches.

Three researchers carried out independent searches. After duplicates were removed, 4,136 studies remained that seemed to be candidates for inclusion based on their titles, abstracts, or topic of focus. Many of these studies were ultimately excluded for: (1) not presenting any statistical associations; (2) not presenting a statistical association between one of our predictor domains and violence, aggression, delinquency, or victimization at school; (3) not specifying that violence, aggression, delinquency, or victimization took place while *at school*; and (4) not presenting enough information to calculate an effect size estimate.[2]

A total of 761 studies spanning over six decades comprised our final sample, and these are listed in the Supplementary Online Appendix. A PRISMA ("Preferred Reporting Items for Systematic Reviews and Meta-Analysis") flow diagram for the screening and inclusion of studies is provided in Appendix B (Moher et al., 2009). The studies contributed a total of 8,790 effect size estimates: 3,879 (44.1 percent) for school violence, aggression, and delinquency, and 4,911 (55.9 percent) for school victimization. The studies were based on samples from seventy-two different nations, with the majority of effect size estimates (56.1 percent) drawn from US samples. Most effect sizes were based on samples of middle school students (22.3 percent), high school students (18.1 percent), or a combination of the two (23.3 percent), whereas a smaller portion were drawn from samples of elementary school students (20.0 percent), a combination of elementary and middle school students (12.8 percent), or students from a wider range of grade levels (K–12; 3.5 percent). Outcomes were measured primarily through self-reports (76.4 percent), but also included peer (14.6 percent), teacher (7.6 percent), and parent reports (0.9 percent), research observations (0.4 percent), and administrative reports (0.2 percent).

Because of the broad inclusion criteria, the sample of studies encompasses a wide spectrum of violent, aggressive, and delinquent acts. Doing so is important for both theoretical and practical purposes when it comes to offending and victimization at school. Theoretically, there is a well-documented pattern in

---

[2] In studies where there was not sufficient information to calculate an effect size estimate, school violence was not the focal variable, and thus the models treating school violence as an outcome were described only briefly in the text or in footnotes. In others, effect sizes could not be calculated because standard errors for unstandardized regression coefficients were not reported, standard errors for odds ratios were not presented, or means were provided without standard deviations.

the criminological literature known as the "generality of deviance" (Hirschi & Gottfredson, 1994) – that is, the tendency for people who engage in one form of deviant or antisocial behavior to also be willing to engage in others. Criminologists have devoted considerable effort to explaining this phenomenon through the construction of "general" theories – those that conceive the sources of deviant behavior to be the same regardless of the form of behavior in question (Agnew, 2006; Akers, 1998; Gottfredson & Hirschi, 1990; Hirschi, 1969). It is important that our meta-analysis includes studies that examine a wide range of criminal, deviant, and antisocial behaviors so that we can shed light on the extent to which the generality of deviance does, or does not, hold up in the school context.

With respect to victimization, however, there are some theoretical perspectives that view the sources of certain forms of violence as essentially unique – particularly those that involve a power imbalance between the offender and the victim. For example, scholars have argued that the sources of minor forms of interpersonal aggression (e.g., verbal bullying and peer victimization) are potentially distinct from more serious forms of interpersonal violence (e.g., physical assaults, weapon use), which are themselves different from gender-based forms of violence and victimization (e.g., sexual assault and harassment, see Conroy, 2013; Reid & Sullivan, 2009; Ybarra et al., 2014). It is therefore critical to examine whether the correlates of different forms of school victimization are roughly the same or if they differ from one form of victimization to the next. Such information carries practical weight as well, since "general" risk factors may be targeted by interventions that could conceivably impact a wide array of violent behaviors at school, whereas evidence that different forms of violence and victimization have unique correlates would indicate the need for more targeted and tailored interventions.

In total, the effect size estimates reflect bullying perpetration (27.9 percent), bullying victimization (33.4 percent), violent offending (6.6 percent), violent victimization (11.1 percent), nonviolent offending (2.5 percent), nonviolent victimization (5.9 percent), bringing a weapon to school (4.4 percent), exposure to violence (1.1 percent), general delinquency (2.7 percent), and general interpersonal victimization (4.3 percent). "General" delinquency and victimization categories reflect those instances in the literature where violent and nonviolent items were combined into a single measure. We deemed it important to include forms of nonviolent delinquency and victimization, such as theft and verbal threats, given that these too are aggressive, interpersonal behaviors that can be distressing to students, parents, teachers, and school administrators. An overview of the sample of effect size estimates for school violence perpetration (including violent, aggressive, and delinquent

Table 1 Overview of effect size estimates for school violence
perpetration

Characteristic	Percent	*N*
Type of outcome		
Bullying	63.21	2,452
Violent offending	15.03	583
General violence	2.71	105
Assault	9.62	373
Aggravated assault	0.26	10
Sexual aggression	2.47	95
Nonviolent offending	5.57	216
General nonviolent	0.95	37
Theft	0.28	11
Threats	4.33	168
General delinquency	6.16	239
Bringing a weapon to school	10.03	389
Predictor domains		
Individual domains		
Age	6.65	258
Sex (male)	21.63	839
Race (non-white)	4.72	183
Socioeconomic status	3.92	152
Self-control	2.99	116
Deviant peers	1.80	70
Antisocial attitudes	5.83	226
Antisocial behavior	15.70	609
Substance use	1.83	71
Bonds to parents	3.61	140
Bonds to school	4.00	155
Academic achievement	2.68	104
Extracurricular activities	0.46	18
Risk avoidance	0.54	21
Victimization	8.12	315
Peer rejection	2.14	83
Popularity	1.99	77
Social competence	4.18	162
LGBT identification	1.01	39
Disability (physical or learning)	1.93	75
School domains		
Negative school climate	1.80	70

Table 1 (cont.)

Characteristic	Percent	N
Violent school context	0.28	11
School disorder	0.46	18
Urban school	0.46	18
School size	0.39	15
Community domains		
Economic deprivation	0.21	8
Community crime	0.54	21
Community disorder	0.13	5
Research design		
Bivariate	60.81	2,359

$N = 3,879$ effect size estimates across 456 studies.

behaviors) is provided in Table 1, and an overview of the sample for victimization is provided in Table 2.

2.4 Predictor Domains

Effect size estimates were coded and grouped into thirty different predictor domains that reflect features of individuals, schools, and communities.[3] The term "predictor domain" is used in meta-analysis to refer to a similar set of independent variables, or "predictors," that are assessed within primary studies (Bonta et al., 1998; Gendreau et al., 1996; Pratt et al., 2010). Because the measurement of key concepts varies across the literature (e.g., there are various ways to measure self-control, bonds to school, and socioeconomic status), similar constructs are grouped into "domains." Consistent with an ecological framework, we recognize that school violence can be "multiply-determined and multiply-influenced" by individual, family, peer, school, community, and cultural factors (Swearer & Espelage, 2011, p. 5). Accordingly, we include a range

---

[3] Before coding began, a protocol was developed to explicitly outline the coding of each predictor domain and effect size estimate in the meta-analysis. Developing a protocol was important to minimize ambiguity in coding decisions and ensure uniformity in coding across studies. The coding scheme was piloted on a random sample of ten studies before the formal coding process began to check for and resolve any problems. Interrater reliability was assessed at the outset using four studies and sixty effect size estimates and was calculated at 0.88 across four separate coders. Interrater reliability assessed toward the end of the coding process across four studies and fifty-two effect size estimates was calculated at 0.98 for the two remaining coders. Throughout the coding process, any questions that arose in coding decisions were discussed and resolved collectively among multiple coders. For accuracy and reproducibility, 500 studies were double-coded by two members of the research team.

Table 2 Overview of effect size estimates for school victimization

Characteristic	Percent	*N*
Type of outcome		
Bullying victimization	59.78	2,936
Violent victimization	19.93	979
General violence	5.01	246
Assault	8.49	417
Aggravated assault	0.96	47
Sexual aggression	5.48	269
Nonviolent victimization	10.72	522
General nonviolent	1.71	84
Theft	3.91	192
Threats	5.01	246
General interpersonal victimization	7.76	381
Exposure to violence	1.89	93
Predictor domains		
Individual domains		
Age	6.48	317
Sex (male)	20.63	1009
Race (non-white)	7.46	365
Socioeconomic status	3.82	187
Self-control	1.37	67
Deviant peers	0.78	38
Antisocial attitudes	1.84	90
Antisocial behavior	9.94	486
Substance use	1.17	57
Bonds to parents	2.04	100
Bonds to school	4.42	216
Academic achievement	4.07	199
Extracurricular activities	1.98	97
Risk avoidance	0.57	28
Weapon carrying	0.43	21
Prior/other victimization	10.18	500
Peer rejection	2.36	116
Popularity	0.65	32
Social competence	4.13	203
LGBT identification	2.65	130
Disability (physical or learning)	3.12	153
School domains		
Negative school climate	3.32	163

Table 2 (cont.)

Characteristic	Percent	N
Violent school context	1.14	56
School disorder	1.12	55
Urban school	1.08	53
School size	1.91	94
Security devices	0.31	15
Community domains		
Economic deprivation	1.04	51
Community crime	0.26	13
Research design		
Bivariate	60.58	2,975

$N = 4,911$ effect size estimates across 550 studies.

of predictor domains that tap into individual characteristics (e.g., demographic, behavioral, social, and experiential risk and protective factors), school characteristics (e.g., school size, security, and climate), and features of the communities in which students and schools are embedded (e.g., economic deprivation).

We emphasize, however, that we cannot establish causal relationships between the various predictor domains and school violence in the meta-analysis. This is due largely to the fact that causality cannot be determined within the primary studies themselves. Indeed, 87.5 percent of the effect size estimates in the meta-analysis reflect cross-sectional (rather than longitudinal) associations, and very few studies used advanced statistical modeling or quasi-experimental designs. The relationships that are presented between predictor domains and school violence should thus be interpreted only as correlations, and not causal associations.

2.4.1 Individual Predictor Domains

Beginning with individual demographic correlates, we included *age, sex* (male), *race* (non-white), and *socioeconomic status*. Socioeconomic status (SES) could include composite measures related to overall SES, as well as individual indicators, such as parental education, affluence, parental occupation, or income (Tippett & Wolke, 2014).

Individual criminological risk factors included *self-control, deviant peers, antisocial attitudes, antisocial behavior, substance use, bonds to parents*, and *bonds to school*. Self-control was conceptualized broadly to include measures of impulsivity, impulse control, sensation-seeking, and risk-seeking (de Ridder et al., 2012). Deviant peers included having friends or spending time with peers that engage in deviance or that hold deviance-promoting attitudes; and antisocial attitudes generally captured students' agreement to statements about the acceptability or rationalization of aggression and violence (Ousey & Wilcox, 2005). Antisocial behaviors were defined to encompass delinquency, aggression, and violence, on or off school property; and substance use could include smoking, drinking, and drug use. Bonds to parents and to school captured various dimensions of attachment, commitment, and involvement (Hirschi, 1969), and bonds to parents also included parental control measures (Hoeve et al., 2012).

Academic achievement, extracurricular activities, risk avoidance behaviors, weapon carrying, and *victimization* were also included. Academic achievement was measured using indicators such as grades, grade-point average, class rankings, and test scores (where higher scores reflected greater academic achievement). Extracurricular activities could include involvement in student clubs, school sports, student organizations, and other related activities (Popp & Peguero, 2011). Risk avoidance captured behaviors such as staying away from school generally or avoiding certain students or places at school due to fear of being harmed (Randa & Wilcox, 2012); and weapon carrying indicated whether students brought a gun, knife, or some other weapon to school (Goldstein et al., 2008). Weapon carrying was assessed only in relation to victimization, since there were too few effect sizes to examine weapon carrying with respect to violent and aggressive behaviors. As a predictor domain, victimization could include violent and nonviolent acts of harm or abuse sustained on or off school property.

To shed light on social dynamics, we also assessed *peer rejection, popularity,* and *social competence.* Peer rejection was defined broadly to include active dislike and social exclusion by peers. Popularity could include self-report, sociometric, and perceived popularity measures, such as peer likability nominations and number of friends (Slaughter et al., 2015). Although related, peer rejection and popularity are distinct constructs (Bellmore, 2011). Social competence was measured using social competency indices, metrics of social skills, social functioning, and social adaptability. Broadly defined, social competence refers to effectiveness in social interaction (Rose-Krasnor, 1997).

Lastly, we included *LGBT identification* and *disability* at the individual level. LGBT identification could include lesbian, gay, bisexual, and transgender students; and disability status encompassed physical, intellectual, and learning disabilities. Measures of disability status in the literature ranged from global indicators (e.g., any disability) to more specific measures of physical limitations, craniofacial problems, attention deficit hyperactivity disorder (ADHD), autism spectrum disorder, sensory disorder, and emotional-behavioral disorders.

2.4.2 School Predictor Domains

School characteristics included *negative school climate, violent school context, school disorder, urban school, school size,* and *school security devices.* Negative school climate captured various indices that tapped into perceptions of the school environment as hostile, unfriendly, or unwelcoming; such as the school having unclear or unfair rules; or the school having negative teacher, staff, or student interactions (Bae, 2016; Carbone-Lopez et al., 2010; Rinehart & Espelage, 2016). Violent school context included measures of violence and victimization at the school level, as well as student perceptions about how common or how much of a problem violence was at school. School disorder was defined by indicators related to perceptions of social and physical disorder at school, such as gang activity, fights, drug and alcohol use, graffiti, trash, and other signs of disorder (Peguero & Jiang, 2016).[4] Urban school reflected whether schools were located in city centers, or urban versus suburban or rural areas; and school size captured the size of the student body. School security devices could include visible security measures, such as the presence of metal detectors and security cameras at school (Tanner-Smith & Fisher, 2016). The presence of school security devices was assessed for victimization only, given that there were too few effect sizes to examine in relation to aggressive and delinquent behaviors.

2.4.3 Community Predictor Domains

At the community level, *economic deprivation, community crime,* and *community disorder* were included. Economic deprivation included concentrated

---

[4] School predictor domains were coded from studies that varied in their multilevel designs. Specifically, with respect to domains of school climate, violent school context, and school disorder, there were studies that assessed school perceptions of these factors among individuals (e.g., Astor et al., 2006; Carbone-Lopez et al., 2010; Goldstein et al., 2008; Juvonen et al., 2016; Moon & Alarid, 2015), and others that aggregated individual perceptions to the school level (e.g., Attar-Schwartz, 2009; Zaykowski & Gunter, 2012). Some studies also included both school- and individual-level measures to aid in the interpretation of school-level contextual effects (e.g., Gottfredson & DiPietro, 2011). The meta-analysis was inclusive of all of these effect size estimates. Supplemental analyses revealed no statistically significant differences in mean effect size estimates for school climate, violent school context, or school disorder depending on whether individual versus aggregate level measures were used, or whether the effect size was derived from a multilevel model (e.g., hierarchical linear modeling). The only exception was for school victimization, where the mean effect size for school climate was reduced if it was derived from a multilevel model.

disadvantage and poverty in the communities where students or schools were embedded. Community crime encompassed violent and nonviolent crime, and neighborhood safety (Schreck et al., 2003); and community disorder captured various signs of physical and social disorder, such as vacant housing, urban degradation, rundown buildings, and neighborhood drug problems (Bacchini et al., 2009; Boggess, 2016; Forrest et al., 2000). Community disorder was assessed in relation to aggressive and delinquent behaviors, but not victimization, due to too few effect sizes.

2.5 Effect Size Estimates

Effect size estimates were measured using correlation coefficients (r) and standardized regression slopes obtained from the quantitative results reported in each of the 761 studies described earlier. Correlation coefficients are bivariate estimates that were typically obtained from correlation matrices or calculated from descriptive statistics presented in each study; and standardized regression slopes were obtained or calculated from multivariate statistical models. Such effect sizes can be interpreted as the change in the dependent variable (school violence) associated with a standard deviation change in the independent variable. These effect size metrics were chosen not only for their ease of interpretation but also because formulas were widely available for converting other test statistics into an r value. Such flexibility is useful in the present literature where various statistical methods are employed across studies. For example, when standardized slopes were not available, effect sizes could be calculated from reported test statistics using $r = t/\sqrt{t^2 + n - 2}$ and $r = z/\sqrt{z^2 + n}$ (see Ousey & Kubrin, 2018; Pratt et al., 2014). Using Fisher's r to z transformation, the effect size estimates were converted into a $z(r)$ score (Hedges & Olkin, 1985). Coefficients were converted into z values since the sampling distribution of $z(r)$ scores is assumed to approach normality. This method can be applied to both bivariate and multivariate effect sizes (Pyrooz et al., 2016; Wolfe & Lawson, 2020).[5]

Both bivariate and multivariate (or "partial") effect sizes were included in the meta-analysis. Even though it is common to use both types of effect sizes in criminological meta-analyses (e.g., see Baier & Wright, 2001; Paternoster, 1987; Pratt & Cullen, 2005; Pratt et al., 2014), it can still be a contentious issue, as each type of effect size estimate has its limitations. On the one hand, the potential downside of using bivariate estimates is that of failing to account for

---

[5] To guard against the slight positive bias that could be produced by Fisher's r to z transformation (Hedges & Olkin, 1985), effect size estimates were first adjusted using the following formula: $r_i = r - [r(1 - r^2)/2(n - 3)]$. Fisher's r to z transformation is as follows: $z(r_i) = \frac{1}{2}\ln[(1 + r_i)/(1 - r_i)]$.

partial spuriousness. Since the influences of other predictors on the dependent variable have not been removed, the bivariate correlation risks being inflated. And while standardized coefficients from multivariate models may produce more valid effect size estimates than the bivariate coefficients (because the issue of spuriousness has already been dealt with), a drawback of using multivariate effect sizes is that they can vary widely within and across studies according to the ways in which statistical models are specified (Aloe et al., 2016; Lipsey & Wilson, 2001). In our sample, approximately 60 percent of effect size estimates were bivariate, and 40 percent were multivariate. Rather than limit our meta-analysis to only one set of effect size estimates, we include both, and adjust the results to account for the proportion of bivariate and multivariate effect size estimates present within each sample (described later).

2.6 Analytic Strategy

The analyses were carried out separately for school violence perpetration and for victimization. For each set of analysis, we first calculated mean effect size estimates for all of the predictor domains, and then ranked them in terms of their magnitude. Next, analyses were conducted to determine whether the mean effect size estimates were stronger or weaker for particular forms of school violence (bullying, violent offending, nonviolent offending, general delin-quency, and bringing a weapon to school) and school victimization (bullying, violent victimization, nonviolent victimization, general victimization, and exposure to violence). Collectively, these analyses provide information on the strength and generality of effects for each predictor domain on school violence perpetration and victimization.

To estimate mean effect sizes for the predictor domains, we used multilevel modeling (Turanovic & Pratt, 2021). This strategy was appropriate given that the data were structured hierarchically, such that effect sizes were nested within individual studies. The data were structured this way because most studies in the meta-analysis contributed more than one effect size estimate to the sample. Indeed, most studies presented multiple statistical relationships – for different forms of school violence, for different predictor domains, across different model specifications, or separately for different groups of students. We opted to code multiple effect sizes per study, per predictor domain, since it would be difficult to develop a defensible decision rule for selecting just one effect size estimate while ignoring others from the same study. Doing so could introduce a "researcher bias" into the meta-analysis (Pratt & Cullen, 2000, p. 941).

Although more traditional approaches to meta-analysis suggest eliminating statistical dependence from the data – such as by selecting only one effect size per study or per outcome, averaging effect sizes within studies, or performing separate meta-analyses on different subsets of the data (e.g., Gleser & Olkin, 1994; Rosenthal & Rubin, 1986) – methods have since advanced, and multilevel modeling techniques allow for researchers to retain as much information as possible in the data in the form of multiple effect size estimates per study (Becker, 2000; Turanovic & Pratt, 2021; van den Noortgate et al., 2013). According to Moeyaert and colleagues (2017, p. 571), multilevel meta-analysis is a "valid and efficient" way to handle dependent effect sizes within a study, without requiring estimates of the correlations between effect sizes.

In the context of meta-analysis, multilevel models explicitly recognize that effect sizes from the same study can be more similar than effect sizes from other studies, and that some studies contribute more effect sizes than others (Raudenbush & Bryk, 2002). By incorporating a unique random effect for each group (i.e., study) into the statistical model, multilevel modeling proced-ures avoid violating the assumption of independent observations that traditional regression analysis would commit if applied to nested data. In addition, due to the parameter estimates not being independent in these models, a study that reports ten effect size estimates will not contribute to the meta-analysis ten times more than a study reporting just one effect size. Rather, the reliability of effect size estimates within groups (i.e., studies) is used to estimate the variance of group-level parameters. The more reliable the effect size estimates are within a particular group, the greater the weight that is assigned to the group mean. Likewise, the less reliable the estimates are in a group, the smaller the weight that is assigned to the group mean.

To calculate mean effect size estimates, we used a special form of multilevel modeling – the "variance known" model – designed for meta-analytic data (Raudenbush & Bryk, 2002). This modeling strategy was necessary since a portion of the variance in effect size estimates is known. We accounted for this variance by calculating standard errors for each effect size estimate, using information reported in each study.

Following prior research, bivariate standard errors were calculated using $\sigma = \sqrt{1/(n-3)}$ (see Lipsey & Wilson, 2001), and multivariate standard errors were calculated using $\sigma = r/(b/SE)$, where b is the unstandardized regression coefficient and SE is the corresponding standard error as reported in the primary studies (Pratt et al., 2014; Pyrooz et al., 2016; Wolfe & Lawson, 2020). Variance-known models were specified by including the standard error of effect size estimates in the random part of the level 1 equation with a constrained variance of one (Hox, 2010). All models adjusted for differences between bivariate and multivariate effect sizes by using a grand mean centered indicator. By grand mean centering this variable, the model intercept reflects the mean effect size adjusted for the proportion of multivariate versus bivariate effect sizes in each sample (see Park, 2008; Raudenbush & Bryk, 2002).[6] The analyses were carried out in Stata 16 using *meglm* (StataCorp, 2019). In what follows, we present the results of these analyses – first for the perpetration of school violence (in Section 3) and then for victimization (in Section 4).

3 Results for School Violence Perpetration

In this section, we present and describe the meta-analytic results for the perpetration of school violence, aggression, and delinquency. First, mean effect sizes for each predictor domain are presented. Consistent with prior meta-analyses (Pratt & Cullen, 2005), we rank order the mean effect sizes by magnitude and identify the strongest risk and protective factors. Next, we assess the generality of relationships by determining whether the mean effect size estimates vary across different outcome types (bullying, violent offending, nonviolent delinquency, general delinquency, and bringing a weapon to school). We conclude by summarizing the results and highlighting the predictor domains that are most strongly and consistently related to the perpetration of violence, aggression, and delinquency at school.

3.1 Strength of Predictor Domains

Table 3 displays the rank order of the mean effect sizes for school violence perpetration across 3,879 effect sizes and 456 studies. The rank ordering of these predictor domains was based on the relative magnitude of the mean effect sizes presented in Table 4.

The predictor domain that was related most strongly to school violence, aggression, and delinquency was antisocial behavior. This mean effect size was above 0.50, which is substantial. This estimate was also based on a large number of contributing effect sizes (609), which gives us further confidence in its strength.[7] Recall that antisocial behavior was measured broadly to encompass various forms of deviance, aggression, and externalizing problems occurring in or out of school. As a result, effect sizes for antisocial behavior were drawn from studies that

---

[6] As an alternative to this approach, in supplemental analyses we also (1) controlled for the number of covariates in the model from which each effect size was drawn, and (2) controlled for the type of statistical model from which each effect size was drawn. None of these approaches led to different conclusions or changed the relative rankings of the predictor domains.

[7] A small number of effect sizes for antisocial behavior in the data were large in magnitude and reflected near-perfect correlations with school violence perpetration. Postestimation tests were thus conducted to confirm that the mean effect size calculated for antisocial behavior was not the product of these outliers. After removing outlier observations from the data (identified using deviance and Anscombe residuals), the resulting mean effect size for antisocial behavior was 0.5043. This is similar in magnitude to the mean effect size of 0.5064 presented in Table 4, indicating that the mean effect size is not sensitive to outliers.

Table 3 Rank-ordered predictor domains for school violence perpetration

Rank	Predictor domain	Rank	Predictor domain
1	Antisocial behavior	16	Negative school climate
2	Deviant peers	17	Violent school context
3	Victimization	18	LGBT identification
4	Antisocial attitudes	19	Community disorder
5	Peer rejection	20	Race (non-white)
6	Substance use	21	School size
7	Social competence (-)	22	Socioeconomic status
8	Self-control (-)	23	Age
9	Bonds to parents (-)		
10	Disability (physical or learning)		
11	School disorder	*n.s.*	Extracurricular activities
12	Bonds to school (-)	*n.s.*	Risk avoidance
13	Academic achievement (-)	*n.s.*	Popularity
14	Community crime	*n.s.*	Urban school
15	Sex (male)	*n.s.*	Economic deprivation

Note: Rank ordering is based on the magnitude of mean effect size estimates presented in Table 4. Predictor domains negatively associated with aggression and delinquency at school are indicated by (-).

n.s. indicates that there was no statistically significant relationship between the predictor domain and violent, aggressive, or delinquent behaviors at school.

examined relationships between different forms of aggression at school (such as the correlations between physical, verbal, and relational aggression); from studies that examined associations between violence, aggression, or delinquency outside and inside of school; and from studies that examined patterns of antisocial behavior over time (such as how strongly youths' involvement in violence during one school year was correlated with the next year).

Accordingly, the large mean effect size for antisocial behavior likely reflects three broad patterns. First, youths are prone to be "generalists" rather than "specialists" when it comes to antisocial behaviors at school, where they rarely engage in just one specific form of violence, aggression, or delinquency (DuRant et al., 1997). Second, youths who engage in antisocial behaviors outside of school (on the streets, at home, or online) are also more likely to engage in antisocial behaviors inside of school (Wei et al., 2010). And third, among youths, past antisocial behavior is associated with future antisocial behavior at school (Jambon & Smetana, 2018).

The next five predictor domains that ranked in the upper quartile of the distribution were deviant peers, victimization, antisocial attitudes, peer

Table 4 Mean effect size estimates for school violence perpetration

Predictor domain	Mean ES	(SE)	95% CI	N (ES)	N (studies)
Individual domains					
Age^	0.0221*	(0.0088)	0.0049 – 0.0392	258	99
Sex (male)^	0.1109***	(0.0064)	0.0984 – 0.1234	839	276
Race (non-white)^	0.0426*	(0.0185)	0.0064 – 0.0788	183	56
Socioeconomic status^	−0.0367***	(0.0112)	−0.0587 – −0.0147	152	48
Self-control^	−0.1643***	(0.0302)	−0.2234 – −0.1052	116	27
Deviant peers	0.2260***	(0.0327)	0.1619 – 0.2900	70	19
Antisocial attitudes^	0.2256***	(0.0160)	0.1944 – 0.2569	226	48
Antisocial behavior^	0.5064***	(0.0227)	0.4620 – 0.5508	609	152
Substance use^	0.2032***	(0.0171)	0.1698 – 0.2367	71	17
Bonds to parents^	−0.1596***	(0.0224)	−0.2036 – −0.1157	140	144
Bonds to school^	−0.1388***	(0.0131)	−0.1645 – −0.1132	155	49
Academic achievement^	−0.1282***	(0.0137)	−0.1551 – −0.1013	104	43
Extracurricular activities	0.0087	(0.0300)	−0.0501 – 0.0675	18	10
Risk avoidance	−0.0001	(0.0476)	−0.0934 – 0.0932	21	7
Victimization^	0.2258***	(0.0152)	0.1961 – 0.2556	315	102
Peer rejection	0.2078***	(0.0464)	0.1168 – 0.2988	83	18

	ES	SE	CI		
Popularity	-0.0408	(0.0460)	-0.1309 – 0.0493	77	16
Social competence	-0.1691***	(0.0279)	-0.2238 – -0.1144	162	55
LGBT identification	0.0896***	(0.0170)	0.0562 – 0.1230	39	6
Disability	0.1511**	(0.0482)	0.0566 – 0.2455	75	17
School domains					
Negative school climate	0.1068***	(0.0260)	0.0557 – 0.1578	70	28
Violent school context^	0.1039***	(0.0062)	0.0918 – 0.1161	11	5
School disorder^	0.1431***	(0.0149)	0.1138 – 0.1724	18	2
Urban school^	-0.0047	(0.0166)	-0.0372 – 0.0278	18	8
School size	-0.0396**	(0.0117)	-0.0625 – -0.0166	15	7
Community domains					
Economic deprivation	-0.0402	(0.0784)	-0.1938 – 0.1134	8	3
Community crime	0.1251**	(0.0313)	0.0638 – 0.1864	21	8
Community disorder	0.0692***	(0.0169)	0.0361 – 0.1024	5	2

Notes: Effect sizes are Fisher z transformed. Mean effect sizes were estimated using variance-known hierarchical linear models, with intercepts adjusted for the proportion of bivariate versus multivariate effect sizes.

Abbreviations: CI = confidence interval; ES = mean effect size; SE = standard error.

^ bivariate and multivariate effect sizes differ in magnitude ($p < 0.05$).

* $p < 0.05$; ** $p < 0.01$; *** $p < 0.001$ (two-tailed test).

rejection, and substance use. Each had a mean effect size above 0.20 and was positively associated with school violence, aggression, and delinquency. The strong relationships observed for deviant peers and antisocial attitudes were consistent with social learning theory (Akers, 1998), and the robust association for victimization was not unexpected given the large literature on the victim–offender overlap (Berg & Mulford, 2020). The mean effect size for peer rejection is notable and larger than several other traditional criminological covariates (e.g., self-control, bonds to parents, bonds to school). Substantively, it indicates that youths who are rejected, excluded, or alienated by their peers are more likely to act out violently or aggressively at school.

The domains ranked from seven to seventeen were more moderate in magnitude, with mean effect size estimates under 0.20 but above 0.10. Included here were social competence, self-control, bonds to parents, disability, school disorder, bonds to school, academic achievement, community crime, sex (male), negative school climate, and violent school context. Some of these factors were negatively (or inversely) associated with outcomes of school violence, indicating that youths with higher social competence, higher self-control, stronger bonds to parents and to school, and higher academic achievement were *less* likely to engage in school violence, aggression, and delinquency.

The predictor domains ranked from eighteen to twenty-three had weak associations with school violence perpetration, with mean effect size estimates under 0.10. Effect sizes this small are generally considered by meta-analysts to be "substantively unimportant" (Pratt & Cullen, 2005, p. 399). Included in this group were LGBT identification, community disorder, race (non-white), school size, socioeconomic status, and age. Lastly, there were also several predictor domains that had null associations with school violence perpetration: extracurricular activities, risk avoidance, popularity, urban school, and economic deprivation. These weak and null results reveal a few noteworthy patterns. For one, several of the criminogenic characteristics of communities in which students and schools are embedded – which may well be strong correlates of crime on the streets – appear to be weakly associated with violence, aggression, and delinquency within schools. Second, routine activity measures that have previously been associated with delinquency, such as involvement in extracurricular activities, had an almost nonexistent association with school violence perpetration, and a mean effect size that was close to zero. Third, individual demographic characteristics that tend to be consistently correlated with criminal behavior – race, age, and socioeconomic status – were not strong correlates of school violence perpetration.

To better interpret the strength of predictor domains in relation to one another, a forest plot of the mean effect size estimates is presented in Figure 1. To the right of the distribution are those predictor domains that had positive

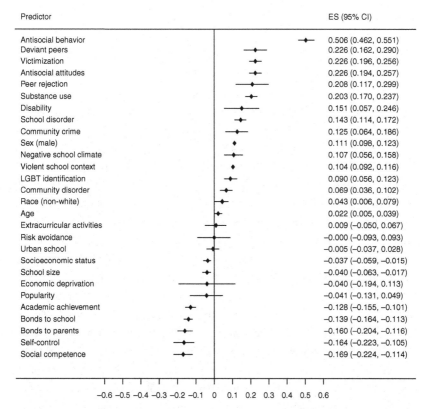

Predictor   ES (95% CI)

Antisocial behavior	0.506 (0.462, 0.551)
Deviant peers	0.226 (0.162, 0.290)
Victimization	0.226 (0.196, 0.256)
Antisocial attitudes	0.226 (0.194, 0.257)
Peer rejection	0.208 (0.117, 0.299)
Substance use	0.203 (0.170, 0.237)
Disability	0.151 (0.057, 0.246)
School disorder	0.143 (0.114, 0.172)
Community crime	0.125 (0.064, 0.186)
Sex (male)	0.111 (0.098, 0.123)
Negative school climate	0.107 (0.056, 0.158)
Violent school context	0.104 (0.092, 0.116)
LGBT identification	0.090 (0.056, 0.123)
Community disorder	0.069 (0.036, 0.102)
Race (non-white)	0.043 (0.006, 0.079)
Age	0.022 (0.005, 0.039)
Extracurricular activities	0.009 (−0.050, 0.067)
Risk avoidance	−0.000 (−0.093, 0.093)
Urban school	−0.005 (−0.037, 0.028)
Socioeconomic status	−0.037 (−0.059, −0.015)
School size	−0.040 (−0.063, −0.017)
Economic deprivation	−0.040 (−0.194, 0.113)
Popularity	−0.041 (−0.131, 0.049)
Academic achievement	−0.128 (−0.155, −0.101)
Bonds to school	−0.139 (−0.164, −0.113)
Bonds to parents	−0.160 (−0.204, −0.116)
Self-control	−0.164 (−0.223, −0.105)
Social competence	−0.169 (−0.224, −0.114)

−0.6 −0.5 −0.4 −0.3 −0.2 −0.1 0 0.1 0.2 0.3 0.4 0.5 0.6

Figure 1 Forest plot for school violence perpetration
Abbreviations: CI = confidence interval; ES = mean effect size.

associations with school violence perpetration, and to the left are those that had negative (or inverse) associations. The further away from zero (to the right or to the left), the stronger the mean effect size. The predictor domains with confidence intervals that include zero are not statistically significant. As seen in the top right of the figure, antisocial behavior stands out from the rest of the distribution as the strongest correlate assessed.

3.2 Generality of Effects

After having ranked the strength of predictor domains, the next step in the analysis was to examine the generality of effects across the different forms of school violence, aggression, and delinquency in the literature. Specifically, we determined whether the effect size estimates for each predictor domain were stable across the following five different outcome categories: (1) bullying; (2) violent offending; (3) nonviolent offending; (4) general delinquency; and (5) bringing a weapon to school. A categorical variable was included in each model to assess whether certain outcome types were more strongly associated with the effect sizes than others.

To generate findings for ten possible comparisons between the five categories, we ran four iterations of our model with different categories as the reference group. Predictor domains that were deemed as having "generality" across outcomes were those whereas the clear majority of comparisons (at least eight out of a possible ten) were not statistically significant ($p > 0.05$). Alternatively, predictor domains that varied significantly across three or more comparisons ($p < 0.05$) were flagged as having mean effect sizes that were not general but specific to particular forms of school violence perpetration.[8] The results of these analyses are summarized in the rightmost columns of Table 5. The vast majority of predictor domains exhibited generality across all forms of school violence, aggression, and delinquency, where just five did not. The five that varied by outcome type included antisocial behavior, victimization, sex (male), negative school climate, and socioeconomic status.

More specifically, antisocial behavior and victimization – which were ranked 1 and 3, respectively, in terms of their overall strength – were more weakly associated with bringing a weapon to school than the other outcomes of school violence, aggression, and delinquency. The analyses indicated that the mean effect size for antisocial behavior on weapon carrying was 0.170, whereas the mean effect sizes were close to three-times higher (or more) for antisocial behavior on the other outcomes: bullying (0.546); violent offending (0.504); nonviolent offending (0.582); and general delinquency (0.586). Likewise, the mean effect size for victimization on weapon carrying was 0.099, which was much weaker than the mean effect sizes for victimization on bullying (0.247), violent offending (0.251), nonviolent offending (0.248), and general delinquency (0.282).

The other three predictor domains that did not exhibit generality were those that already had weak to moderate associations with school violence, aggression, and delinquency. The results showed that the effect size for sex (male) was smaller for bullying, that negative school climate was a stronger correlate of general delinquency relative to the other outcomes, and that socioeconomic status was a weaker correlate of nonviolent offending.

3.3 Summary of Findings

The meta-analytic results presented thus far reveal a few important patterns. For one, antisocial behavior has by far the strongest association with school

---

[8] Comparisons were also evaluated using adjusted levels of statistical significance based on the false discovery rate (FDR) correction (Benjamini & Hochberg, 2000). The FDR correction is an alternative to the traditional Bonferroni approach and controls for the expected proportion of falsely rejected hypotheses due to multiple comparisons. Regardless of whether we used adjusted or unadjusted p-values, our inferences about generality remained the same.

Table 5 Strength and generality of effects for school violence perpetration

	Relative strength				Generality	
Predictor domain	Strong	Moderate	Weak	Null	Yes	No
Antisocial behavior	✓					✓
Deviant peers	✓				✓	
Victimization	✓					✓
Antisocial attitudes	✓				✓	
Peer rejection	✓				✓	
Substance use	✓				✓	
Social competence		✓			✓	
Self-control		✓			✓	
Bonds to parents		✓			✓	
Disability		✓			✓	
School disorder		✓			✓	
Bonds to school		✓			✓	
Academic achievement		✓			✓	
Community crime		✓			✓	
Sex (male)		✓				✓
Negative school climate		✓				✓
Violent school context		✓			✓	
LGBT identification			✓		✓	
Community disorder			✓		✓	
Race (non-white)			✓		✓	
School size			✓		✓	
Socioeconomic status			✓			✓
Age			✓		✓	
Risk avoidance				✓	✓	
Extracurricular activities				✓	✓	
Popularity				✓	✓	
Urban school				✓	✓	
Economic deprivation				✓	✓	

violence perpetration, indicating: (1) that youths who partake in antisocial behaviors outside of school engage in similar behaviors inside of school; (2) that past behavior is a strong correlate of future behavior; and (3) that youths are versatile when it comes to the types of aggression, delinquency, or violence that they commit at school. Antisocial behavior was, however, more weakly associated with bringing a weapon to school relative to the other outcomes (bullying, violent offending, nonviolent offending, and general delinquency), suggesting that weapon carrying may be more difficult to predict based on youths' past behaviors or participation in other forms of school aggression or delinquency.

Second, deviant peers and antisocial attitudes had some of the strongest associations with school violence perpetration, and their effect sizes were general across all forms of delinquency and aggression that we assessed. From the perspective of social learning theory, these patterns reflect the components of *differential association* and *definitions* (Akers, 1998). That is, through differential association with deviant peers, youths can learn definitions favorable to deviance, be exposed to deviant behavioral models, and receive social reinforcement for engaging in deviant behavior. Antisocial attitudes refer to the definitions that individuals attach to antisocial behavior. The more that youths define antisocial behavior as good, permissible, and excusable – and the less they define it as bad and negative – the more likely they are to engage in it (see also Bonta & Andrews, 2017).

Third, and similar in strength to deviant peers, victimization was a robust correlate of school violence, aggression, and delinquency. As such, youths who have been bullied, abused, or harassed – either at school, at home, on the streets, or online – are more likely to harm other students and engage in destructive behaviors at school. But relative to the other outcomes assessed, victimization was not strongly associated with bringing a weapon to school. It may be that weapon carrying is shaped more by factors other than one's victimization experiences, such as deviant peer influences and antisocial attitudes.

Fourth, peer rejection was among the top five strongest correlates of school violence perpetration. Its mean effect size outweighed those of more traditional criminological correlates – such as self-control, bonds to parents, bonds to school, and academic achievement. Its effect sizes were also general and stable across all outcomes, indicating that it is a robust correlate of school bullying, violent and nonviolent offending, general delinquency, and bringing a weapon to school.

Lastly, there were several predictor domains that had null and weak associations with school violence perpetration, despite their relationship to crime and deviance more generally. These included demographic factors (socioeconomic status, race, and age), community characteristics (economic deprivation and community disorder), and extracurricular activities. We also did not find evidence that school size or school urbanicity were meaningfully associated with the perpetration of school violence.

4 Results for School Victimization

Next, we shift our focus to school victimization. This section proceeds as follows. First, we present mean effect sizes for each predictor domain and rank order them by magnitude to identify the strongest risk and protective factors for victimization at school. After that, we discuss the generality of effects across different types of school victimization (bullying, violence, victimization, nonviolent victimization, general victimization, and exposure to violence at school). We conclude with a summary of key findings and draw attention to the predictor domains that were most strongly and consistently related to victimization at school.

4.1 Strength of Predictor Domains

Table 6 displays the rank order of the mean effect sizes for school victimization across 4,911 effect sizes and 550 studies. The rank ordering of these predictor domains is based on the relative magnitude of the mean effect size estimates presented in Table 7.

The top correlate of school victimization was prior/other victimization, with a large mean effect size of 0.465. This estimate is particularly robust, given that it was based on a sizeable sample (500).[9] Keep in mind that the measure of prior/ other victimization was broad and inclusive, and it captured various experiences with victimization occurring in schools, homes, and communities. Effect sizes were drawn from studies that examined associations between victimization inside and outside of school; from studies that assessed the links between different types of victimization at school; and from studies that examined patterns of school victimization over time. Given the breadth of the prior/ other victimization measure, there are likely three key explanations for its large mean effect size. First, youths who are victimized or bullied outside of school – such as online, at home, or on the streets – are also likely to be victimized in school (Juvonen & Gross, 2008). Second, youths who are victimized at school are unlikely to be subjected to just one form of aggression or violence. Rather, they may experience multiple forms of victimization, such as physical, verbal, *and* relational abuse by other students (Salmivalli et al., 2011). And third, past victimization is a robust correlate of future victimization – meaning that once youths are victimized at school, they are at greater risk of being victimized again (Wilcox, May, et al., 2006).

The second strongest predictor domain for school victimization was social competence, which had a negative mean effect size, and was just above the absolute value of 0.30. This effect size was noteworthy since it outweighed the more traditional risk factors of victimization that are often emphasized in the criminological literature (e.g., antisocial behavior, deviant peers, substance use,

---

[9] Postestimation tests revealed that the large mean effect size for prior/other victimization was not an artifact of outliers. After removing outlier observations from the data (identified using deviance and Anscombe residuals), the mean effect size estimate was 0.4619, which is similar in magnitude to the effect size of 0.4651 presented in Table 7.

Table 6 Rank-ordered predictor domains for school victimization

Rank	Predictor domain	Rank	Predictor domain
1	Prior/other victimization	16	Bonds to parents (-)
2	Social competence (-)	17	Antisocial attitudes
3	Risk avoidance	18	Weapon carrying
4	Antisocial behavior	19	Deviant peers
5	Peer rejection	20	School disorder
6	Negative school climate	21	Sex (male)
7	Community crime	22	Age (-)
8	LGBT identification	23	Economic deprivation
9	Violent school context	24	School size
10	Disability (physical or learning)	25	Socioeconomic status (-)
11	Bonds to school (-)		
12	Academic achievement (-)	*n.s.*	Race (non-white)
13	Popularity (-)	*n.s.*	Extracurricular activities
14	Self-control (-)	*n.s.*	Urban school
15	Substance use	*n.s.*	Security devices

Notes: Rank ordering is based on the mean effect size estimates presented in Table 7. Predictor domains negatively associated with school victimization are indicated by (-).
n.s. indicates that there was no statistically significant relationship between the predictor domain and school victimization.

self-control). Still, the strong and negative mean effect size indicates that it is an important protective factor, whereby youths who have higher levels of social competence – demonstrated by characteristics such as strong social skills and high social functioning – are less likely to be victimized at school (Egan & Perry, 1998).

Following social competence, the next three strongest mean effect size estimates (ranked from three to five) were risk avoidance, antisocial behavior, and peer rejection. All had positive associations with victimization, with mean effect sizes that hovered below 0.25 and above 0.23. The positive mean effect size for antisocial behavior was consistent with the literature on the victim–offender overlap, confirming that youths who engage in antisocial behavior face greater risks of school victimization (Ousey et al., 2008). The effect size for peer rejection on victimization was similar in magnitude to that of antisocial behavior, indicating that youths who are socially isolated or excluded by their peers are more likely to be victimized at school.

Table 7 Mean effect size estimates for school victimization

Predictor domain	Mean ES	(SE)	95% CI	N (ES)	N (Studies)
Individual domains					
Age	-0.0480***	(0.0071)	-0.0620 – -0.0340	317	108
Sex (male)	0.0581***	(0.0067)	0.0450 – 0.0714	1,009	314
Race (non-white)	-0.0127	(0.0081)	-0.0286 – 0.0032	365	90
Socioeconomic status^	-0.0141*	(0.0058)	-0.0254 – -0.0028	187	54
Self-control	-0.0973**	(0.0301)	-0.1563 – -0.0383	67	22
Deviant peers	0.0686***	(0.0182)	0.0330 – 0.1042	38	15
Antisocial attitudes^	0.0859***	(0.0162)	0.0542 – 0.1176	90	22
Antisocial behavior^	0.2370***	(0.0124)	0.2127 – 0.2614	486	156
Substance use	0.0954**	(0.0343)	0.0281 – 0.1627	57	17
Bonds to parents^	-0.0938***	(0.0179)	-0.1289 – -0.0587	100	41
Bonds to school^	-0.1215***	(0.0089)	-0.1389 – -0.1041	216	66
Academic achievement^	-0.1157***	(0.0187)	-0.1525 – -0.0790	199	65
Extracurricular activities^	-0.0123	(0.0105)	-0.0328 – 0.0082	97	24
Risk avoidance^	0.2424***	(0.0372)	0.1695 – 0.3152	28	8
Weapon carrying^	0.0778***	(0.0165)	0.0454 – 0.1101	21	7
Prior/other victimization^	0.4651***	(0.0242)	0.4178 – 0.5125	500	122

Table 7 (cont.)

Predictor domain	Mean ES	(SE)	95% CI		N (ES)	N (Studies)
Peer rejection^	0.2326***	(0.0471)	0.1402 –	0.3250	116	31
Popularity^	–0.1072*	(0.0410)	–0.1875 –	–0.0269	32	9
Social competence	–0.3004***	(0.0227)	–0.3450 –	–0.2559	203	68
LGBT identification^	0.1618***	(0.0180)	0.1265 –	0.1972	130	29
Disability	0.1366***	(0.0308)	0.0762 –	0.1969	153	19
School domains						
Negative school climate^	0.1777***	(0.0177)	0.1430 –	0.2125	163	45
Violent school context^	0.1537***	(0.0366)	0.0819 –	0.2254	56	15
School disorder^	0.0619***	(0.0096)	0.0431 –	0.0808	55	12
Urban school	–0.0099	(0.0061)	–0.0219 –	0.0021	53	17
School size	–0.0199*	(0.0080)	–0.0355 –	–0.0041	94	28
Security devices	–0.0031	(0.0083)	–0.0193 –	0.0130	15	6
Community domains						
Economic deprivation^	0.0336**	(0.0123)	0.0095 –	0.0577	51	16
Community crime^	0.1681***	(0.0012)	0.1657 –	0.1704	13	5

Notes: Effect sizes are Fisher z transformed. Mean effect sizes were estimated using variance-known hierarchical linear models, with intercepts adjusted for the proportion of bivariate versus multivariate effect sizes.

Abbreviations: CI = confidence interval; ES = mean effect size; SE = standard error.

^ bivariate and multivariate effect sizes differ in magnitude ($p < 0.05$).

* $p < 0.05$; ** $p < 0.01$; *** $p < 0.001$ (two-tailed test).

Although risk avoidance had a strong and positive association with victimization, we caution against interpreting this effect size as evidence that risk avoidance *increases* the risk of victimization at school. Rather, the magnitude and direction of the mean effect size likely reflects the cross-sectional nature of most primary studies, and that youths take efforts to avoid people or places at school *because* they have been victimized (Benbenishty et al., 2002). Indeed, several studies presented cross-sectional associations between school victimization and risk avoidance, including group differences in avoidance behaviors between victims and nonvictims, where time ordering between victimization and risk avoidance could not be sufficiently established (Bauman, 2008; Meyer-Adams & Conner, 2008; Welsh, 2001).

The predictor domains ranked from six to thirteen were more moderate in magnitude, with mean effect sizes under 0.20 but above 0.10. The strongest correlates in this group were negative school climate, community crime, LGBT identification, violent school context, and disability. Recall that negative school climate, community crime, and violent school context (ranked number six, seven, and nine, respectively) were contextual correlates, and they reflect characteristics of schools and communities (or perceptions of schools and communities) that shape students' risks of victimization. LGBT identification and disability were ranked number eight and ten, respectively, suggesting that students may experience victimization at school as a result of cultural biases and prejudicial beliefs surrounding sexual orientation, gender identity, and physical and learning impairments (Myers et al., 2020; Twyman et al., 2010). The predictor domains ranked eleven through thirteen were all negatively associated with school victimization and had effect sizes closer to −0.10, indicating that youths with stronger bonds to school, higher academic achievement, and greater popularity were less likely to be victimized.

The predictor domains ranked from fourteen to twenty-five represent weak predictors of school victimization, with effect size estimates under 0.10. These include self-control, substance use, bonds to parents, antisocial attitudes, weapon carrying, deviant peers, school disorder, sex (male), age, economic deprivation, school size, and socioeconomic status. There were also four predictor domains with null effects, indicating that they were unrelated to victimization at school: race (non-white), extracurricular activities, urban school, and school security devices.

There are a few patterns worth pointing out from these weak and null results. For one, several factors linked with risky lifestyles and youth victimization on the streets – namely, self-control, substance use, antisocial attitudes, weapon carrying, and deviant peer associations (Turanovic & Pratt, 2014) – appear to be poor predictors of victimization at school. Relatedly, the routine activity measure of extracurricular activities had no meaningful association with school victimization. We also found no evidence that "target hardening" practices within schools – in this case, the use of school security devices, such as metal detectors – had any association with school victimization. In fact, the predictor domain of school security devices was the weakest of all, with a mean effect size that was null and virtually zero.

To help convey the relative strength of predictor domains, a forest plot of the mean effect sizes is provided in Figure 2. Recall that the further away from zero (to the left or to the right), the stronger the mean effect size; and that a confidence interval that includes zero signifies a null effect. As can be seen in the figure, prior/other victimization (on the top right) and social competence (on the bottom left) stand out as having the strongest two mean effect sizes in the distribution.

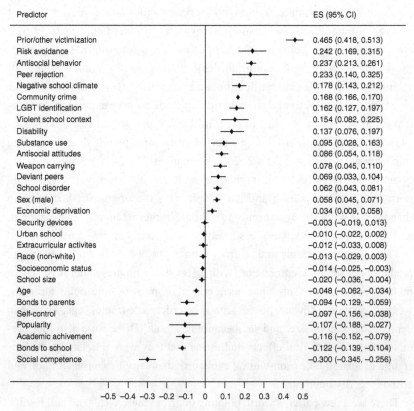

Predictor	ES (95% CI)
Prior/other victimization	0.465 (0.418, 0.513)
Risk avoidance	0.242 (0.169, 0.315)
Antisocial behavior	0.237 (0.213, 0.261)
Peer rejection	0.233 (0.140, 0.325)
Negative school climate	0.178 (0.143, 0.212)
Community crime	0.168 (0.166, 0.170)
LGBT identification	0.162 (0.127, 0.197)
Violent school context	0.154 (0.082, 0.225)
Disability	0.137 (0.076, 0.197)
Substance use	0.095 (0.028, 0.163)
Antisocial attitudes	0.086 (0.054, 0.118)
Weapon carrying	0.078 (0.045, 0.110)
Deviant peers	0.069 (0.033, 0.104)
School disorder	0.062 (0.043, 0.081)
Sex (male)	0.058 (0.045, 0.071)
Economic deprivation	0.034 (0.009, 0.058)
Security devices	−0.003 (−0.019, 0.013)
Urban school	−0.010 (−0.022, 0.002)
Extracurricular activites	−0.012 (−0.033, 0.008)
Race (non-white)	−0.013 (−0.029, 0.003)
Socioeconomic status	−0.014 (−0.025, −0.003)
School size	−0.020 (−0.036, −0.004)
Age	−0.048 (−0.062, −0.034)
Bonds to parents	−0.094 (−0.129, −0.059)
Self-control	−0.097 (−0.156, −0.038)
Popularity	−0.107 (−0.188, −0.027)
Academic achivement	−0.116 (−0.152, −0.079)
Bonds to school	−0.122 (−0.139, −0.104)
Social competence	−0.300 (−0.345, −0.256)

−0.5 −0.4 −0.3 −0.2 −0.1 0 0.1 0.2 0.3 0.4 0.5

Figure 2 Forest plot for school victimization
Abbreviations: CI = confidence interval; ES = mean effect size.

4.2 Generality of Effects

The next step in the analysis was to assess the generality of effects across different forms of victimization at school. Specifically, we assessed whether the effect sizes for each predictor domain were stable across the following five types of school victimization: (1) bullying; (2) violent victimization; (3) nonviolent victimization; (4) general victimization; and (5) exposure to violence. Consistent with the methodological approach described previously in Section 3, a categorical variable for outcome type was included in each model to assess whether the predictor domains were more strongly linked to certain forms of school victimization than others.

To generate findings for ten possible comparisons between the five outcome types, four iterations of our model were estimated, each with a different category as the reference group. Predictor domains that were deemed as having "generality" across outcomes were those where the clear majority of comparisons (at least eight out of a possible ten) were not statistically significant ($p > 0.05$). Alternatively, predictor domains that varied significantly across three or more comparisons ($p < 0.05$) were flagged as having effect sizes that were not general but specific to particular forms of victimization at school.[10]

The results of these analyses are summarized in the rightmost columns of Table 8. As shown, the majority of predictor domains exhibited generality across all forms of school victimization, where just seven of the twenty-nine did not. Note that the top five strongest correlates of victimization at school – prior/other victimization, social competence, risk avoidance, antisocial behavior, and peer rejection – had effect sizes that were general across all forms of victimization. The seven domains with mean effect sizes that varied by outcome type included negative school climate, community crime, violent school context, academic achievement, antisocial attitudes, sex (male), and age.

For the predictor domains of negative school climate, community crime, and violent school context – which were ranked number six, seven, and nine in strength, respectively – the patterns of variability were similar in that each was more strongly associated with exposure to violence than it was with other types of school victimization. For example, the mean effect size for negative school climate on exposure to violence was 0.240 but the mean effect sizes were much weaker for bullying victimization (0.156), violent victimization (0.152), and property victimization (0.144). Similarly, the mean effect size for violent school

---

[10] Comparisons evaluated using FDR-corrected *p*-values did not alter any of our conclusions regarding generality.

Table 8 Strength and generality of effects for school victimization

Predictor domain	Relative strength				Generality	
	Strong	Moderate	Weak	Null	Yes	No
Prior/other victimization	✓				✓	
Social competence	✓				✓	
Risk avoidance	✓				✓	
Antisocial behavior	✓				✓	
Peer rejection	✓				✓	
Negative school climate		✓				✓
Community crime		✓				✓
LGBT identification		✓			✓	
Violent school context		✓				✓
Disability		✓			✓	
Bonds to school		✓			✓	
Academic achievement		✓				✓
Popularity		✓			✓	
Self-control			✓		✓	
Substance use			✓		✓	
Bonds to parents			✓		✓	
Antisocial attitudes			✓			✓
Weapon carrying			✓		✓	
Deviant peers			✓		✓	
School disorder			✓		✓	
Sex (male)			✓			✓
Age			✓			✓
Economic deprivation			✓		✓	
School size			✓		✓	
Socioeconomic status			✓		✓	
Race (non-white)				✓	✓	
Extracurricular activities				✓	✓	
Urban school				✓	✓	
Security devices				✓	✓	

context on exposure to violence was 0.283, which was markedly stronger than the mean effect sizes for violent school context on bullying victimization (0.128), violent victimization (0.155), property victimization (0.150), and general victimization (0.109).

The remaining four predictor domains that did not exhibit generality were those that already had weak associations with victimization at school. The results showed that academic achievement was a weaker correlate of exposure to violence relative to the other outcomes, that the effect sizes for antisocial attitudes and age were stronger for exposure to violence, and that the effect sizes for sex (male) were stronger for violent victimization and weaker for bullying victimization.

4.3 Summary of Findings

From the results presented in this section, a few key findings are worth highlighting. First, the predictor domain of prior/other victimization was the strongest correlate of victimization at school. Consequently, this means: (1) that youths who have been victimized in the past are at risk of being victimized again; (2) that youths who have experienced victimization in other contexts (at home, on the streets, online) are also likely to be victimized at school; and (3) that youths who suffer victimization at school tend to experience it in multiple forms (e.g., physical, verbal, and relational victimization). The effect sizes for prior/other victimization were also consistent across all outcomes, indicating that it is a strong and stable correlate of school bullying victimization, violent and nonviolent victimization, general victimization, and exposure to violence at school.

Second, social competence emerged as a robust protective factor – one that was outmatched in strength only by prior/other victimization. Children high in social competence – characterized by effectiveness in social interactions, adaptability across social contexts, and the ability to maintain positive relationships with others (Rose-Krasnor, 1997) – are far less likely to experience victimization at school. By extension, this means that youths low in social competence – kids who do not have strong social skills, who have difficulty taking the perspective of others, and who struggle with being collaborative and helpful (Englund et al., 2000) – are at risk of being targeted and harassed at school. Relatedly, peer rejection also emerged as a top risk factor for school victimization and had a mean effect size similar in strength to antisocial behavior. The overall strength and generality of effects for social competence and peer rejection emphasize the importance of sociability and peer group dynamics in shaping risks for victimization at school.

Third, antisocial behavior was ranked as the fourth strongest correlate of victimization at school, behind social competence and risk avoidance, and just ahead of peer rejection. Recall that antisocial behavior was a broad measure that included various forms of aggressive and deviant behaviors, ranging from minor to serious delinquency, occurring on or off school grounds (Melde & Esbensen, 2009). The relatively strong mean effect size for antisocial behavior is consistent with the victim–offender overlap and criminological research that demonstrates that youths who are likely to be victimized at school also tend to engage in delinquency (Ousey et al., 2008; Tillyer et al., 2018; Zaykowski & Gunter, 2012). Still, the overlap is far from perfect, and the magnitude of the effect size suggests that engagement in antisocial behavior does not always coincide with school victimization.

Lastly, outside of antisocial behavior, traditional correlates of victimization on the streets – such as those factors that align with the lifestyle-opportunity framework – did not perform well. Specifically, self-control, substance use, antisocial attitudes, weapon carrying, deviant peers, and extracurricular activities were weak or null predictors of victimization at school. Other factors that had weak or null associations to school victimization, despite their links to street victimization, included demographic characteristics (sex (male), age, race, socioeconomic status), bonds to parents, and economic deprivation. Relatedly, the presence of security devices was unrelated to victimization at school and had an effect size that was basically zero. These findings and their implications are discussed in more detail in the following section.

5 Discussion

Understanding the sources of school violence and victimization is a challenging task. Since scholars approach these problems from various academic disciplines (criminology, psychology, education, sociology, social work, and public health), they tend to focus on different outcomes (behaviors ranging from bullying/harassment to physical violence and assaults) and emphasize different correlates (developmental factors versus those associated with opportunities for violence and victimization). Adding to this wide variation in how studies are conducted and where they can be found is the virtual explosion of research on school violence in recent years. But the only way for hundreds of studies to reveal anything useful about which factors do and do not "matter" is to get serious about making sense of what this body of work reveals. That was the purpose of this Element: to undertake a rigorous, comprehensive meta-analysis of this full body of research.

In this section, we discuss the synthesis of 761 studies and 8,790 effect size estimates in several parts. First, we summarize the results in terms of the relative strength of effects for all of the predictor domains of school violence perpetration and victimization, noting which had correlations that were consistently strong, which were consistently weak, and which seemed to be either general or unique across perpetration and victimization. Second, we recognize methodological limitations of the meta-analysis that can be improved in future research. Third, we review the implications of our findings in terms of the need for the development and revision of existing criminological perspectives on school violence, as well as the directions that the next generation of research should consider taking. And finally, we discuss the policy implications stemming from this work that can help guide effective interventions for school violence.

5.1 Strong Correlates

First, there were several factors that stood out as strong correlates of school violence perpetration and victimization. Antisocial behavior and prior/other victimization were at the top of the list, with effect sizes that were consistently strong in magnitude. The effect size for antisocial behavior on the perpetration of school violence, aggression, and delinquency was 0.506 and for school victimization it was 0.237. Likewise, the effect size for victimization on the perpetration of school violence was 0.226, and for school victimization it was 0.465. Effect sizes of this magnitude suggest that youths with histories of victimization and involvement in crime or deviance are at the highest risk for perpetrating and experiencing school violence. As mentioned earlier, predictors of antisocial behavior and prior/other victimization were measured in a variety of ways across studies. Questions therefore remain about which types of antisocial behavior or victimization are most consequential to predicting school violence and victimization (e.g., prior involvement in minor deviance versus serious aggression; victimization in the home versus bullying online).

Another universally strong correlate was peer rejection, which had a mean effect size that was ranked in the top five for perpetration (0.208) and for victimization (0.233). These relationships were found to be general across all forms of violence, aggression, delinquency, and victimization that we assessed. The strength and generality of the effect size estimates were notable in no small part because peer rejection outranked many traditional theoretical correlates commonly considered in criminological research. Yet, peer rejection can influence school violence in a number of ways. With respect to perpetration, scholars suggest that it can be a form of strain that elicits criminal coping (Higgins et al., 2011), or that it can lead rejected youths to act out because they lack the social support from peers needed for healthy development (Thoits, 2011). Others have noted that peer rejection can lead to hostile cognitive bias, where rejected youths interpret ambiguous situations as threatening and respond with aggression (DeWall et al., 2009). Still others contend that with few other friendship options, rejected youths form ties to antisocial peers who end up influencing their behaviors (Kornienko et al., 2020). On the victimization side of things, rejected youths are thought to be more vulnerable targets because they have few friends to defend or protect them (Cook, Williams, et al., 2010), and they tend to occupy a marginalized social status (Juvonen & Graham, 2014). Keeping these various explanations in mind, we recommend that peer rejection be central to the study of school violence moving forward.

Another consistent correlate of both perpetration and victimization was social competence. And while the mean effect size was much stronger for victimization (−0.300) than it was for violence, aggression, and delinquency (−0.169), these correlations stand out. Specifically, for all types of school violence perpetration (bullying, violent and nonviolent offending, general delinquency, and weapon carrying), the results showed that social competence acts as a protective factor. The associations between social competence and school victimization were also stable across all forms of victimization assessed (bullying victimization, violent and nonviolent victimization, general victimization, and exposure to school violence), and the overall effect size was consistent with a prior meta-analysis on bullying victimization (Cook, Williams, et al., 2010). Given that socially competent youths tend to have strong verbal and relational skills, they may avoid victimization by being able to effectively diffuse and deescalate interpersonal disputes (Felson et al., 2018), or they may have more quality friendships with youths who are willing to intervene to protect them from harm (Bukowski et al., 2020). These results suggest that youths who have poor social functioning are at an elevated risk of victimization at school, which likely coincides with their peripheral position in peer groups (Mulvey et al., 2017). In short, with respect to the study of school violence, it is important to consider social competence in the future (Beelmann & Lösel, 2021).

Several factors had more moderate but consistent associations with school violence that are worth calling attention to as well, such as bonds to school (with effect sizes of −0.139 for perpetration and −0.122 for victimization), and physical or learning disabilities (with effect sizes of 0.151 for perpetration and 0.137 for victimization). The results suggest that these factors also play a meaningful role when it comes to school violence and should be considered in subsequent work. Because an array of physical and learning disabilities were assessed, it would be helpful for scholars to further disentangle which disabilities are linked to violence, aggression, and delinquency and which are not (e.g., ADHD versus other learning and physical limitations). And finally, negative school climate (with effect sizes of 0.107 for perpetration and 0.178 for victimization) and violent school context (with effect sizes of 0.104 for perpetration and 0.154 for victimization) were the only school-level factors that emerged as meaningful correlates of both perpetration and victimization. These patterns indicate that contextual factors cannot be dismissed either, and that it may be useful for future work to continue to explore the causal processes underlying *why* these school characteristics matter.

5.2 Correlates Unique to Perpetration and to Victimization

A few factors emerged as strong correlates of school violence perpetration but weak correlates of victimization, such as deviant peers and antisocial attitudes. These two factors – which stem from the social learning perspective (Akers, 1998) – each had a mean effect size of 0.226 on school violence, aggression, and delinquency. The effect sizes for deviant peers and antisocial attitudes that we estimated were on par with those presented in a prior meta-analysis that assessed the empirical status of social learning theory on crime more broadly (Pratt et al., 2010). Based on these findings, it seems safe to assume that the social learning perspective – as a theory of aggressive and criminal behavior – is one that can be generalized to the school context. Interventions for students that target social learning principles may therefore hold promise in reducing the perpetration of violence, aggression, and delinquency at school.

Alternatively, on the victimization side of things, deviant peers and antisocial attitudes were ranked toward the bottom, with effect sizes of 0.069 and 0.086, respectively. Of course, we recognize that the social learning perspective is not a theory of victimization, since victimization is not a "behavior" that can be modeled and reinforced via traditional social learning mechanisms (Turanovic & Young, 2016). Even so, factors such as deviant peers and antisocial attitudes are presumed to increase the exposure to opportunities for victimization (Schreck et al., 2002). Students who associate with deviant peers or hold antisocial attitudes tend to spend more time in risky settings and are more likely to be exposed to potential offenders who victimize them (Turanovic & Pratt, 2014). But the opportunity explanation seems to break down in the school setting, which is a relatively structured environment. Likewise, substance use – which is another risky lifestyle factor thought to influence victimization through similar opportunity-based mechanisms – was also only weakly associated with school victimization (with an effect size of 0.095), despite its more robust association with perpetration (with an effect size of 0.203).

With few exceptions, almost none of the traditional criminological factors that we assessed were strongly related to school victimization, despite their moderate to strong associations with the perpetration of school violence. In fact, social vulnerability factors such as social competence, peer rejection, LGBT identification, and disability were more important correlates of victimization at school than bonds to school, self-control, substance use, bonds to parents, antisocial attitudes, deviant peers, and weapon carrying – factors that are virtual staples of the criminological literature. These patterns suggest that the theoretical perspectives traditionally used to study victimization at school within the field of criminology likely need to be revised and expanded – a point we will return to later.

Lastly, risk avoidance was a strong correlate of school victimization (with an effect size of 0.242) but it had no relationship to school violence, aggression, or delinquency (the effect size was zero). And though we cautioned against interpreting the results as evidence that risk avoidance increases victimization (due to problems with temporal ordering in the primary studies themselves), the results still reveal notable patterns. They indicate that victims of school violence (but not those who perpetrate it) are likely to face higher risks of school disengagement by avoiding going to school, or by staying away from certain places at school, out of fear of being harmed. However, there were only eight studies in the meta-analysis that assessed the relationship between risk avoidance and school victimization. Much more rigorous research is needed before firmer conclusions can be drawn.

5.3 Weak Correlates

Weak correlates of school violence perpetration and victimization included race (non-white), socioeconomic status, urban school, school size, and economic deprivation. These findings were somewhat inconsistent with the literature on crime and violence more generally. For example, broader criminological research has documented that racial/ethnic minorities and those who experience socioeconomic strains are more likely to be victimized or to engage in crime and delinquency, and that urban communities with high concentrations of people, and with more economic deprivation, tend to have higher rates of victimization, crime, and violence (Krivo & Peterson, 1996; Turanovic & Pratt, 2019; Wilcox Rountree et al., 1994). Although prior research has linked some of these contextual correlates to school shootings (Fridel, 2021), collectively, their weak and null associations in this meta-analysis emphasize that school violence – when conceptualized more broadly – is a problem that cuts across racial groups and social classes, and that affects students who attend schools in a wide range of communities, regardless of their levels of disadvantage.

It is also possible, however, that community characteristics influence school violence *indirectly* through factors such as antisocial behavior, victimization, deviant peers, antisocial attitudes, and social competence. To be sure, these problems likely originate in the home or in the community. A wealth of literature suggests that community conditions shape child development, parenting practices, exposure to adversity, and prosocial ties (Legewie & Fagan, 2019; Sampson, 2012; Sharkey, 2010, 2018). So, while many of the contextual factors that we assessed did not have strong, direct associations with school violence or victimization, they likely serve as the *sources* of the factors that do (Bronfenbrenner, 1979; Gaias et al., 2018; Roos et al., 2019).

Additionally, there are more nuanced patterns and conditional effects that should be explored when it comes to certain factors, such as race. Even though we found that race was a weak correlate of school violence and victimization generally, it is possible that this relationship is conditional upon the racial and ethnic composition of schools – namely, whether racial or ethnic groups make up the numerical majority or minority at their school (Juvonen & Graham, 2014). When it comes to victimization, for example, members of smaller minority groups may be viewed as more vulnerable targets because they deviate from the dominant majority group (Bellmore et al., 2004), and because they have fewer same-race/ethnic peers to help ward off potential perpetrators (Hanish & Guerra, 2002). Some research suggests that ethnically diverse classrooms may reduce rates of victimization because the balance of power is shared by various groups (Juvonen et al., 2006). Thus, there are many more avenues to explore with respect to how race, ethnicity, and racial/ethnic diversity in schools shape the risk of violence and victimization.

Another factor that was consistently ranked near the bottom for both perpetration and victimization was extracurricular activities. The routine activity research has generally supported the idea that involvement in structured activities after school (as opposed to unstructured leisure activities) serves to protect students against antisocial behavior (Osgood et al., 2005; Riese et al., 2015), and that activities such as participation in school sports and other school organizations increases the risk of victimization by prolonging the amount of time youths spend with peers in less supervised settings (Cecen-Celik & Keith, 2019; Wilcox et al., 2009). Here, we found little evidence to support these claims with respect to school violence. Instead, the mean effect sizes for extracurricular activities on perpetration and victimization were null. And though we recognize that not every type of extracurricular activity carries similar risks or protections (Feldman & Matjasko, 2005; Peguero, 2008a), in the literature we assessed, the effect sizes for extracurricular activities of various forms were consistently clustered near zero. Even among similar types of activities, such as sports, there were both negative and positive effects sizes produced that were small in magnitude (DuRant et al., 1999; Tillyer et al., 2018; Wilcox et al., 2009). These patterns are not what would be expected if the involvement in extracurricular activities was an important correlate of school violence.

We also found minimal evidence that visible security measures, such as metal detectors and security cameras, had any meaningful associations with school victimization. This is consequential since, in recent years, many schools have increased their use of security devices and have invested in similar target-hardening approaches (Addington, 2009; Schildkraut & Grogan, 2019; Wang et al., 2020). The logic behind doing so comes from deterrence and routine activity theories, which assume that such security measures should deter youths from victimizing others by increasing guardianship and increasing the per-ceived risks of apprehension and punishment (Hollis et al., 2013). But the sources of school violence are more complex than what can be targeted through the use of visible security measures alone (Jonson, 2017; Kupchik, 2016; Tanner-Smith et al., 2018). We caution, therefore, against viewing the target hardening of schools as sufficient for addressing school violence. Still, we were not able to assess security devices in relation to the perpetration of school violence, nor could we evaluate how they were used or enforced, whether they were viewed as legitimate by students, or if they had other impacts on perceptions of school safety (see Johnson et al., 2018; Mowen & Freng, 2019). Such issues should be further explored.

5.4 Limitations

Although several limitations of the meta-analysis have already been discussed – including the inability to establish causal associations – there are three more worth noting. First, as outlined earlier, the technique of meta-analysis is useful for establishing broad patterns. Accordingly, we focused on determining: (1) the relative magnitude of effect sizes; and (2) their generality across different forms of school violence and victimization. What we did not assess was the extent to which the effect size estimates were conditioned by other methodological variations across studies. As noted, the vast majority of effect size estimates reflected cross-sectional (rather than longitudinal) associations, and very few studies used advanced statistical modeling techniques. As school violence research continues to grow and improve, the sensitivity of effect size estimates to different measurement strategies, sampling characteristics, temporal specifi-cations, and modeling approaches should be examined. Doing so will help to further identify which factors are the most robust and stable correlates of school violence and victimization across the literature.

Second, the meta-analysis was based only on studies that measured school violence and victimization at the individual level. There are dozens of studies that examine violence and victimization at the aggregate level – where schools (rather than students) are the unit of analysis – and these were not included. The various school and community characteristics that we assessed (i.e., negative school climate, violent school context, school disorder, urban school, school size, security devices, economic deprivation, community crime, and community disorder) likely have different relationships with school violence and victimization at the school level (Boggess, 2016; Jennings et al., 2011; Na & Gottfredson, 2013). Indeed, between-school variance in school violence may be more relevant than within-school variance for understanding the influences of school- and community-level correlates (Gottfredson & DiPietro, 2011; Gottfredson et al., 2005; Swartz et al., 2017). To better assess contextual effects, a meta-analysis of the aggregate school violence literature may be warranted.

Third, even though a lengthy roster of individual-, school-, and community-level correlates were assessed in the meta-analysis, it was not possible to include all potential risk factors for school violence, aggression, and victimization. Due to too few effect size estimates, we were unable to assess the influence of school resource officers or guards, school disciplinary policies, or other school-level factors (e.g., race and gender composition of schools) in relation to school violence and victimization. We also did not examine immigrant status, which is understudied relative to race and ethnicity. Growing research suggests that immigrant youths are at heightened risk of being victimized and bullied at school (Alivernini et al., 2019; Maynard et al., 2016; Stevens et al., 2020), but the findings are mixed (Peguero, 2008b, 2013; Vitoroulis & Georgiades, 2017). It would be useful for policy and prevention efforts if this research were to be meta-analyzed as well. There were also other risk factors that we did not examine, such as moral disengagement, callous unemotional traits, narcissism, and empathy (Gini et al., 2014; Killer et al., 2019; Zych et al., 2019), which have been linked to school bullying and peer aggression. It is unknown whether these factors would be as strongly related to more serious forms of school violence and delinquency, and this issue should be considered as research progresses.

5.5 Criminological Implications

Taken together, despite the limitations discussed, the findings have several important implications for criminological theory and research on school violence. For one, scholars should be mindful that the etiology of school violence may be different from street violence (Cook, Gottfredson, et al., 2010), given that several traditional criminological predictors did not perform strongly in the school context. The demographic correlates of school violence were different (where race, sex (male), and socioeconomic status were not strongly related to perpetration or victimization), and major theories of offending and victimization – namely, opportunity and control perspectives – did not generalize well to the school setting. Across the board, the effects of self-control and social bonds were modest, and routine activity factors, as noted earlier, were virtually irrelevant. Even risky lifestyle indicators (e.g., deviant peers and substance use) turned out to be weak correlates of victimization at school. Alternatively, factors such as peer rejection and social competence seemed to hold much more promise – and these are components of broader developmental perspectives that emphasize peer hierarchies, social status, and social vulnerability. As a result, peer and social dynamics should be better integrated into the study of violence and victimization at school (Faris & Felmlee, 2014; Faris et al., 2020; Troop-Gordon, 2017). Unless the field expands its horizons to look beyond traditional criminological theories, much of the variation in school violence is likely to remain unexplained.

In advancing this line of work, network-based approaches may be helpful. Such approaches tend to be based on sociological models of group processes – those that recognize that violence and victimization carry social rewards and consequences (Kornienko et al., 2018; Salmivalli, 2010; Troop-Gordon, 2017). Thus far, social network studies of school violence have been useful for understanding how students' positions in their network positions increase (or decrease) vulnerability to victimization, and how perpetrating violence reduces (or enhances) status in school social hierarchies (Dijkstra et al., 2010; Huitsing & Veenstra, 2012; van der Ploeg et al., 2020). Although much of this work suggests that vulnerable, weak, or stigmatized youths – those on the margins of school social networks – tend to be the most likely victims of peer harassment (Merrin et al., 2018; Mouttapa et al., 2004; Veenstra et al., 2007), some research suggests that increases in status also increases the risk of victimization, and that only those youths at the uppermost extremes of school hierarchies avoid victimization (Faris & Felmlee, 2014). Research also shows that aggression can be used to gain status (Sijtsema et al., 2009), and that students who bully their classmates are likely to befriend each other (Rambaran et al., 2020). Still, highly aggressive youths may not be well-liked (Hektner et al., 2000; Sijtsema et al., 2010), and especially among younger children, victims may not be selected very strategically (Huitsing & Monks, 2018). In short, there is much to learn about how social networks facilitate school violence, and this is a fruitful avenue for future research.

Second, greater attention should be devoted to identifying the theoretical mechanisms that link various correlates and risk factors to school violence and victimization. The processes by which key factors influence school violence and its consequences are often "black boxed" and are rarely tested explicitly. For example, the results indicated that antisocial behavior, victimization, and peer rejection were among the strongest correlates of school violence perpetration, yet little research has specified theoretically or measured directly the processes by which these factors are presumed to lead to violence at school. Possible mechanisms may include strain and anger (Agnew, 2006), social learning processes (Akers, 1998), poor interpersonal adjustment (e.g., fear or mistrust), hostile attribution bias (de Castro et al., 2002), reduced empathy for others (Caravita et al., 2009), or diminished self-efficacy (Kokkinos & Kipritsi, 2012). This lack of research knowledge is consequential because, depending on the mechanisms at work, unique treatment and programming approaches may be needed. By identifying the causal processes that link various factors to school violence, more effective programs and policies can be developed (Hirschfield, 2018).

Third, as efforts are made to develop new approaches and perspectives, scholars must recognize that school violence perpetration and victimization are not interchangeable outcomes. While overlap exists among their strongest correlates, they are also influenced by unique sets of factors. This means that victims of school violence and those who perpetrate it are not always the same individuals. Our findings, for instance, suggest that LGBT youths are at moderate risk for school victimization but at lower risk for the perpetration of school violence, aggression, and delinquency. Bullying research for years has recognized these sorts of differences, acknowledging that bullies and victims can be distinct in several ways (Juvonen & Graham, 2014). Some of this work suggests that bullies have low empathy, that they tend to be impulsive, domineering, uncooperative, and high in defensive egotism, and that they often have larger social circles (Brank et al., 2012; Nail et al., 2016). In contrast, victims of bullying tend to be socially anxious, submissive and withdrawn, have fewer close friendships, and seem as though they just "don't fit in" at school (Hoover et al., 1992; Ladd et al., 2019). And while there is certainly overlap between victimization and perpetration to consider (Berg & Mulford, 2020; Rodkin et al., 2015; Veenstra et al., 2005), future research can benefit from a greater appreciation of the various ways in which victims and perpetrators of school violence can be unique from one another. Doing so would again require expanding the theoretical lens through which we study violence at school not to rely too heavily on theories of crime to predict victimization. School violence perpetration and victimization appear to be qualitatively different phenomena, and we will reach a better understanding of both if we respect those differences.

Fourth, and relatedly, subsequent work should examine the extent to which the major risk factors for school violence and victimization vary by age. As youths get older and contend with shifting peer dynamics, biological changes, and an increased awareness of their sexuality, it is possible that the association between some correlates of school violence and victimization intensify, that some weaken, and that other novel risk factors emerge (Cillessen & Lansu, 2015). For instance, status enhancement is particularly important during early adolescence, which coincides with the transition from elementary to middle school (Pellegrini & Long, 2002; Troop-Gordon, 2017). Not only do aggressive behaviors tend to increase during this developmental phase but they also tend to be guided by social dominance motives and a desire for popularity (Juvonen & Graham, 2014) – motives that are not as salient among younger children (LaFontana & Cillessen, 2010). Also, as youths age throughout adolescence, their capacity for empathy increases (Allemand et al., 2014), as does their ability to control their impulses (Forrest et al., 2019), which may influence not only the types of aggression that they engage in but also the types of students that may be targeted. It is thus possible that some risk factors for school violence perpetration and victimization are age-graded, and that the nature of violence among younger students is unique from older students. The developmental changes that occur between early childhood and late adolescence are profound and should be incorporated explicitly into school violence research (Lipsey & Derzon, 1998).

Fifth, as research progresses, there is a need to increase focus on serious forms of violence at school. The overwhelming majority of studies included in the meta-analyses were based on bullying. Studies of serious school violence – particularly involving weapons – were much rarer. The overwhelming focus on bullying may partly explain why factors typically associated with street violence – such as, community economic deprivation – had weak effects throughout the literature. Although many of the strongest correlates had general effects across multiple forms of school violence, there is still much to learn about the extent to which different forms of aggression and violence at school share the same underlying risk factors (Astor et al., 2010), or the extent to which school violence is distinct from youth violence in the community (Swartz et al., 2017). Particularly from a policy perspective, it is unknown whether school programs that target less serious forms of aggression would also hold promise in reducing serious forms of violence, or if specific forms of school violence require their own specialized interventions (Fite et al., 2020). There is a need for researchers to assess a wider spectrum of violent acts, and to conduct studies that provide direct comparisons of the sources of in-school versus out-of-school violence.

Lastly, moving forward, it will also be important for researchers to obtain more detailed information on the situations and contexts surrounding school violence, in addition to students' and teachers' perceptions about the precursors to violent incidents. At present, little is known about the kinds of interactions between students that are most likely to trigger violent responses (Averdijk et al., 2016; Malette, 2017), or the specific settings at school in which different forms of violence, aggression, and delinquency tend to unfold. A situational approach would allow researchers to examine more detailed features of incidents themselves, including immediate contexts and the actions and behaviors of all parties involved (Dong et al., 2020). Such an approach would reveal more about the roles of power differentials between victims and perpetrators (e.g., student gender, race, age, or popularity differences), patterns of escalation or de-escalation, and the conditions under which bystanders either facilitate violence or protect victims from further harm (Ma et al., 2019; Song & Oh, 2017). Of course, advancing a situational approach to school violence would likely require new data collection efforts – including those that are qualitative in nature – to better understand youths' subjective experiences with and involvement in violent incidents. While this may not be an easy task to accomplish, this sort of work could help make major strides toward developing policies and practices that are effective in preventing school violence and victimization.

5.6 Implications for Policy and Practice

The results of the meta-analysis have important implications for policy and practice – especially when it comes to school-based interventions intended to reduce school violence and victimization. In particular, the results point toward three key elements that successful interventions for school violence should carefully consider. The first concerns the factors that interventions should target for change. Given that antisocial behavior, victimization, peer rejection, and social competence were found to be strong correlates of school violence, interventions should incorporate facets of emotional control, conflict management, stress coping, and social skills training. Programs that do so are likely to be successful because they instill and enhance the kinds of socioemotional skills necessary for youths to better navigate peer groups and the social hierarchies that surround them (Beelmann & Lösel, 2021; Dymnicki et al., 2011; Lee et al., 2015). Still, we recommend being cautious of interventions that center *only* on youths, as these may be insufficient at fully addressing the top risk factors for school violence uncovered in the meta-analysis. Instead, interventions should be holistic and inclusive of peers, teachers, school administrators, parents, and the broader neighborhood (Baquedano-López et al., 2013; Lee et al., 2015;

Weisburd et al., 2016). Microsystems of peers (socialization during childhood and adolescence), the family (abuse or neglect, lack of parental monitoring), the school (school climate, teacher attitudes), and the community (exposure to violence) set the stage for violence – and its strongest risk factors – to develop (Espelage, 2014).

Second, the results have implications for the proper mode of service delivery when it comes to interventions for school violence. For instance, since anti-social attitudes and deviant peer influences are strong correlates of school violence perpetration, our results are consistent with the broader intervention literature that suggests cognitive-behavioral programs are likely to be effective (Gaffney et al., 2019; Scheckner et al., 2002). Cognitive-behavioral programs are among the most effective for addressing school violence (Barnes et al., 2014), yet program fidelity is critical, and efforts must be made ahead of time to ensure the readiness of schools to implement a program successfully (Wanless & Domitrovich, 2015). Many school violence interventions are ineffective (Jiménez-Barbero et al., 2016; Merrell et al., 2008), in part because they tend to be comprised of one- or two-day programs that contain little in the way of treatment integrity (Menesini & Salmivalli, 2017). This is not to say that programs need to be ongoing indefinitely, but they do need to have sufficient duration to bring about a meaningful level of cognitive and behavioral change (Astor et al., 2005; Ttofi & Farrington, 2011).

A prime example of the kind of intervention that our results point to is the Seattle Social Development Project – a program implemented across a socioeconomically and racially/ethnically diverse range of eighteen elementary schools in the greater Seattle area, including those located in high-crime neighborhoods (Kim et al., 2016). The intervention was rooted in a social development model that targeted youths' attitudes, behaviors, and social-emotional skill development (e.g., interpersonal problem-solving skills), involved training for teachers in classroom instruction and management (e.g., proactive classroom management and cooperative learning), and included a parenting training component (e.g., behavior management and academic support skills; see Hawkins et al., 2007). The results of the program, which began to roll in during the 1990s, indicated strong and consistent intervention effects across a wide array of important outcomes, including school functioning and performance, emotional and mental health, and school violence and victimization (Herrenkohl et al., 2012; Hill et al., 1999). The program also had lasting effects on problematic behavior and psychological well-being into early adulthood (Hawkins et al., 2005; Lonczak et al., 2002).

Another example of a program that has earned a strong degree of empirical support for reducing school violence and victimization is the Steps to Respect

(STR) program (Frey et al., 2005). Similar to the Seattle Social Development Project, the STR employs a social-ecological approach that views youths' behaviors as being influenced at multiple levels – from individual characteristics, to peer groups, to classrooms, to the broader school environment (Low et al., 2014). The STR's approach to problematic behaviors – which focuses primarily on bullying – includes promoting responsible behaviors and social-emotional skills among students, building friendship skills and increasing protective social connections, instilling appropriate bystander responses to bullying and peer victimization, and teacher and staff trainings regarding classroom monitoring and how to effectively intervene with students (Low et al., 2010). Evaluations of the STR have been consistently positive, indicating that students who participate in the STR curriculum report reduced rates of relational and peer aggression, peer victimization, an improved school climate, and lower levels of self-reported bullying perpetration (Brown et al., 2011).

Other empirically supported programs include the FAST Track program ("Families and Schools Together"), a multicomponent intervention for families and schools that targets children at the highest risk for life-course-persistent conduct problems (Conduct Problems Prevention Research Group, 1992, 2011); the PATHS program ("Promoting Alternative Thinking Strategies"), a classroom-based curriculum to help children develop appropriate problem-solving, self-control, and emotional regulation skills (which has been successfully combined with the FAST Track program; Kusché, 2020; Kusché & Greenberg, 1994); and the Coping Power program, based on a contextual social-cognitive framework, which reduces aggression and improves social competence through interventions with children and parents (Lochman & Wells, 2002).[11]

Despite these promising approaches, there remain substantial roadblocks to effective school violence prevention. A long-standing concern is that many of the known effective strategies for reducing school violence are not implemented nearly as widely as they should be. The failure to scale-up practices that are proven to be effective has been an issue at the forefront of prevention science research for years (Brownson et al., 2017; Spoth et al., 2013; Tibbits et al., 2010). Many communities and schools lack the infrastructures needed to successfully adopt, implement, and sustain evidence-based interventions (Proctor et al., 2009; Woolf, 2008); and stakeholder group preferences, budgetary issues,

---

[11] There are, of course, other examples of effective school violence/bullying interventions that operate at multiple levels – from the student to the teacher to the classroom (Ttofi & Farrington, 2011). These include programs like the Olweus Bullying Prevention Program (Olweus & Limber, 2010; see also Limber, 2011) and the KiVa Antibullying Program (Nocentini & Menesini, 2016; Williford et al., 2012).

support from leadership, and the school organizational climate can enhance or impede the quality of training and prevention activities (Gottfredson et al., 2000). Even at higher organizational levels, there are government budget priorities that can mandate or restrict funding for particular school programs, and these constraints can affect the success and sustainability of evidence-based violence prevention efforts (Ringwalt et al., 2011; Spoth et al., 2013). As research on school violence continues to grow, more evaluations on the scaling-up of programs are needed. Such work can identify the circumstances under which a particular intervention should be adopted, and the ways to improve fit between the intervention, participants, schools, and school districts (Garbacz et al., 2017; Sailor et al., 2021).

Third, our final key point is that, to effectively reduce school violence, schools must move away from adopting punitive, deterrence-based interventions. Perhaps the most widely scaled school safety programs are punishment-oriented and law enforcement-based, which include zero-tolerance mandatory suspension/expulsion policies and the expansion of police officers in schools. In the United States, federal and state governments have allocated millions of dollars of funding for school resource officers (Viano et al., 2021), and zero-tolerance policies are used in most schools in all fifty states (Welch & Payne, 2018). Such approaches often resonate with policy makers, the public, and school administrators because they are rooted in the simple, commonsense assumption that as penalties for misbehavior increase, misbehavior should decrease (Hirschfield, 2008; Kiernan Coon, 2021). And yet, perceptions of increased formal punishments are, at best, only weakly related to offending behavior (Pratt et al., 2006). Hundreds of studies indicate that merely stepping up penalties does little to reduce crime either in (Hirschfield, 2018; Wiley et al., 2020) or out of school (Pratt & Cullen, 2005; Pratt & Turanovic, 2018). Research has yet to even demonstrate that zero-tolerance policies result in greater fairness toward students or more consistent discipline practices (Welch & Payne, 2018).

In fact, there is ample evidence that excessive school punishments carry a host of consequences, (Jacobsen, 2020; Kupchik, 2016; Mowen & Brent, 2016), especially for poor and minority students – including school failure, interpersonal exclusion, dropout, arrest, and incarceration (i.e., the school-to-prison pipeline) – and that such policies can deteriorate the school climate to become *more* hostile and *less* inclusive (Bear et al., 2017; Kupchik & Farina, 2016). The expansion of police officers in schools, too, has resulted in increased punitive responses to discipline problems that are amplified for students of color (Deakin et al., 2018; Homer & Fisher, 2020; Welch & Payne, 2010). The preference for schools and communities to adopt these potentially harmful approaches – especially in lieu of evidence-based interventions that have been demonstrated, using rigorous research, to improve school safety – is a major obstacle to effective school violence prevention. The bottom line is that if we want to take the problems of school violence and victimization seriously, we first need to abandon the idea that more punitiveness is the answer.

5.7 Conclusion

The extraordinary attention given to the welfare of children at school is understandable. It is natural to care about the harm that kids can experience within what is expected to be the safe haven of the schoolhouse. And because we also care about the safety of youths in schools, we felt that our contribution could be to systematically take stock of this remarkable body of literature – via the quantitative methods of meta-analysis – to give a clear empirical account of what is known about the sources of school violence and victimization. Good science, we are convinced, is a means for doing good (Cullen, 2005). Yet, underneath all of the effect size estimates in the data are the lives of children – the human side of the statistics we present. Let us not forget this reality. As the research on school violence continues to grow and improve, so too does the need to put knowledge into practice – to help make schools safe places of support, and not places of harm.

Appendices
Appendix A: Journals Targeted for Additional Searches

1. *Advances in School Mental Health Promotion*
2. *Aggressive Behavior*
3. *American Educational Research Journal*
4. *American Journal of Criminal Justice*
5. *American Journal of Public Health*
6. *American Journal of Sociology*
7. *American Sociological Review*
8. *Anxiety, Stress, and Coping*
9. *Behaviour Research and Therapy*
10. *British Journal of Developmental Psychology*
11. *British Journal of Educational Psychology*
12. *Canadian Journal of School Psychology*
13. *Child Abuse and Neglect*
14. *Child Development*
15. *Child Maltreatment*
16. *Child Welfare*
17. *Children and Youth Services Review*
18. *Clinical Child Psychology and Psychiatry*
19. *Crime & Delinquency*
20. *Criminal Justice and Behavior*
21. *Criminal Justice Review*
22. *Criminal Justice Studies*
23. *Criminology*
24. *Criminology and Criminal Justice*
25. *Development and Psychopathology*
26. *Developmental Psychology*
27. *Developmental Science*
28. *Deviant Behavior*
29. *Educational Psychology*
30. *Educational Research*
31. *Educational Studies*
32. *Emotional and Behavioural Difficulties*
33. *European Journal of Criminology*

34. *European Journal of Developmental Psychology*
35. *International Journal of Adolescence and Youth*
36. *International Journal of Behavioral Development*
37. *International Journal on School Disaffection*
38. *International Review of Victimology*
39. *Journal of Abnormal Child Psychology*
40. *Journal of Adolescence*
41. *Journal of Adolescent Health*
42. *Journal of Adolescent Research*
43. *Journal of Aggression, Maltreatment, and Trauma*
44. *Journal of the American Medical Association*
45. *Journal of the American Medical Association Pediatrics*
46. *Journal of Applied Developmental Psychology*
47. *Journal of Applied School Psychology*
48. *Journal of Child Psychology and Psychiatry*
49. *Journal of Clinical Child and Adolescent Psychology*
50. *Journal of Clinical Psychiatry*
51. *Journal of Community Psychology*
52. *Journal of Consulting and Clinical Psychology*
53. *Journal of Contemporary Criminal Justice*
54. *Journal of Counseling Psychology*
55. *Journal of Crime and Justice*
56. *Journal of Criminal Justice*
57. *Journal of Developmental and Behavioral Pediatrics*
58. *Journal of Early Adolescence*
59. *Journal of Educational and Developmental Psychology*
60. *Journal of Educational Measurement*
61. *Journal of Educational Psychology*
62. *Journal of Emotional and Behavioral Disorders*
63. *Journal of Experimental Child Psychology*
64. *Journal of Evidence Based Social Work*
65. *Journal of Health and Social Behavior*
66. *Journal of Human Behavior in the Social Environment*
67. *Journal of Interpersonal Violence*
68. *Journal of LGBT Youth*
69. *Journal of Pediatric Psychology*
70. *Journal of Pediatrics*
71. *Journal of Personality and Social Psychology*
72. *Journal of Primary Prevention*
73. *Journal of Prevention and Intervention in the Community*

74. *Journal of Quantitative Criminology*
75. *Journal of Research in Crime and Delinquency*
76. *Journal of Research on Adolescence*
77. *Journal of School Health*
78. *Journal of School Psychology*
79. *Journal of School Violence*
80. *Journal of Social and Clinical Psychology*
81. *Journal of the American Academy of Child and Adolescent Psychiatry*
82. *Journal of Traumatic Stress*
83. *Journal of Youth and Adolescence*
84. *Justice Quarterly*
85. *Learning and Instruction*
86. *Maternal and Child Health Journal*
87. *Pediatrics*
88. *Personality and Individual Differences*
89. *Psychology, Health, and Medicine*
90. *Psychology of Violence*
91. *Scandinavian Journal of Psychology*
92. *School Psychology Quarterly*
93. *School Psychology International*
94. *Social Development*
95. *Social Forces*
96. *Social Influence*
97. *Social Networks*
98. *Social Problems*
99. *Social Science Research*
100. *Sociological Focus*
101. *Sociological Spectrum*
102. *Stress, Trauma, and Crisis*
103. *Victims & Offenders*
104. *Violence and Victims*
105. *Youth & Society*
106. *Youth Violence and Juvenile Justice*

Appendix B: PRISMA Flow Diagram

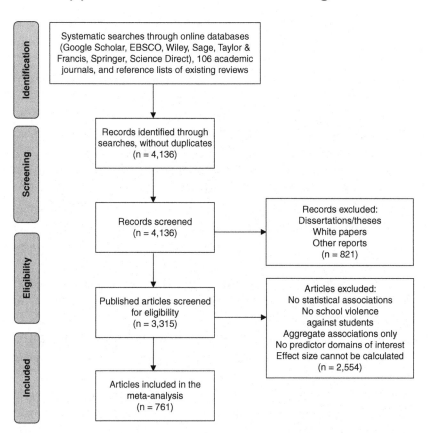

References

Addington, L. A. (2009). Cops and cameras: Public school security as a policy response to Columbine. *American Behavioral Scientist, 52*(10), 1426–46.

Agnew, R. (2006). *Pressured into crime: An overview of general strain theory.* Los Angeles: Roxbury.

Aizpitarte, A., Atherton, O. E., Zheng, L. R., Alonso-Arbiol, I., & Robins, R. W. (2019). Developmental precursors of relational aggression from late childhood through adolescence. *Child Development, 90*(1), 117–26.

Akers, R. L. (1998). *Social learning and social structure: A general theory of crime and deviance.* Boston: Northeastern University Press.

Alivernini, F., Manganelli, S., Cavicchiolo, E., & Lucidi, F. (2019). Measuring bullying and victimization among immigrant and native primary school students: Evidence from Italy. *Journal of Psychoeducational Assessment, 37*(2), 226–38.

Allemand, M., Steiger, A. E., & Fend, H. A. (2014). Empathy development in adolescence predicts social competencies in adulthood. *Journal of Personality, 83*(2), 229–41.

Aloe, A. M., Tanner-Smith, E. E., Becker, B. J., & Wilson, D. B. (2016). Synthesizing bivariate and partial effect sizes. *Campbell Systematic Reviews, 12*(1), 1–9.

Arseneault, L., Bowes, L., & Shakoor, S. (2010). Bullying victimization in youths and mental health problems: "Much ado about nothing"? *Psychological Medicine, 40*(5), 717–29.

Arsenio, W. F., & Lemerise, E. A. (2001). Varieties of childhood bullying: Values, emotion processes, and social competence. *Social Development, 10*(1), 59–73.

Astor, R. A., Benbenishty, R., Haj-Yahia, M. M., et al. (2002). The awareness of risky peer group behaviors on school grounds as predictors of students' victimization on school grounds: Part II – Junior high schools. *Journal of School Violence, 1*(3), 57–76.

Astor, R. A., Benbenishty, R., Vinokur, A. D., & Zeira, A. (2006). Arab and Jewish elementary school students' perceptions of fear and school violence: Understanding the influence of school context. *British Journal of Educational Psychology, 76*(1), 91–118.

Astor, R. A., Guerra, N., & van Acker, R. (2010). How can we improve school safety research? *Educational Researcher, 39*(1), 69–78.

Astor, R. A., Meyer, H. A., Benbenishty, R., Marachi, R., & Rosemond, M. (2005). School safety interventions: Best practices and programs. *Children and Schools*, *27*(1), 17–32.

Attar-Schwartz, S. (2009). Peer sexual harassment victimization at school: The roles of student characteristics, cultural affiliation, and school factors. *American Journal of Orthopsychiatry*, *79*(3), 407–20.

Averdijk, M., van Gelder, J. L., Eisner, M., & Ribeaud, D. (2016). Violence begets violence ... but how? A decision-making perspective on the victim-offender overlap. *Criminology*, *54*(2), 282–306.

Bacchini, D., Esposito, G., & Affuso, G. (2009). Social experience and school bullying. *Journal of Community & Applied Social Psychology*, *19*(1), 17–32.

Bae, H. O. (2016). Bullying involvement of Korean children in Germany and in Korea. *School Psychology International*, *37*(1), 3–17.

Baier, C. J., & Wright, B. R. (2001). "If you love me, keep my commandments": A meta-analysis of the effect of religion on crime. *Journal of Research in Crime and Delinquency*, *38*(1), 3–21.

Baker, J. A. (1998). Are we missing the forest for the trees? Considering the social context of school violence. *Journal of School Psychology*, *36*(1), 29–44.

Baquedano-López, P., Alexander, R. A., & Hernandez, S. J. (2013). Equity issues in parental and community involvement in schools: What teacher educators need to know. *Review of Research in Education*, *37*(1), 149–82.

Barnes, T. N., Smith, S. W., & Miller, M. D. (2014). School-based cognitive-behavioral interventions in the treatment of aggression in the United States: A meta-analysis. *Aggression and Violent Behavior*, *19*(4), 311–21.

Bauman, S. (2008). Victimization by bullying and harassment in high school: Findings from the 2005 Youth Risk Behavior Survey in a southwestern state. *Journal of School Violence*, *7*(3), 86–104.

Bear, G. G., Yang, C., Mantz, L. S., & Harris, A. B. (2017). School-wide practices associated with school climate in elementary, middle, and high schools. *Teaching and Teacher Education*, *63*, 372–83.

Becker, B. J. (2000). Multivariate meta-analysis. In H. E. A. Tinsley & S. D. Brown (eds.), *Handbook of applied multivariate statistics and mathematical modeling* (pp. 499–526). San Diego, CA: Academic Press.

Becker, G. S. (1968). Crime and punishment: An economic approach. *Journal of Political Economy*, *76*(2), 169–217.

Beelmann, A., & Lösel, F. (2021). A comprehensive meta-analysis of randomized evaluations of the effect of child social skills training on antisocial development. *Journal of Developmental and Life-Course Criminology*, *7*(1), 41–65.

Bellmore, A. (2011). Peer rejection and unpopularity: Associations with GPAs across the transition to middle school. *Journal of Educational Psychology*, *103*(2), 282–95.

Bellmore, A. D., Witkow, M. R., Graham, S., & Juvonen, J. (2004). Beyond the individual: The impact of ethnic context and classroom behavioral norms on victims' adjustment. *Developmental Psychology*, *40*(6), 1159–72.

Benbenishty, R., Astor, R. A., & Astor, R. (2005). *School violence in context: Culture, neighborhood, family, school, and gender.* New York: Oxford University Press.

Benbenishty, R., Astor, R. A., Zeira, A., & Vinokur, A. D. (2002). Perceptions of violence and fear of school attendance among junior high school students in Israel. *Social Work Research*, *26*(2), 71–87.

Benjamini, Y., & Hochberg, Y. (2000). On the adaptive control of the false discovery rate in multiple testing with independent statistics. *Journal of Educational and Behavioral Statistics*, *25*(1), 60–83.

Berg, M. T., & Mulford, C. F. (2020). Reappraising and redirecting research on the victim–offender overlap. *Trauma, Violence, & Abuse*, *21*(1), 16–30.

Blake, J. J., Zhou, Q., Kwok, O. M., & Benz, M. R. (2016). Predictors of bullying behavior, victimization, and bully-victim risk among high school students with disabilities. *Remedial and Special Education*, *37*(5), 285–95.

Blau, J. R., & Blau, P. M. (1982). The cost of inequality: Metropolitan structure and violent crime. *American Sociological Review*, *47*(1), 114–29.

Boggess, L. N. (2016). Racial and ethnic change and serious student offending in Los Angeles middle and high schools. *Crime & Delinquency*, *62*(5), 669–700.

Bonta, J., & Andrews, D. A. (2017). *The psychology of criminal conduct* (sixth ed.). New York: Routledge.

Bonta, J., Law, M., & Hanson, K. (1998). The prediction of criminal and violent recidivism among mentally disordered offenders: A meta-analysis. *Psychological Bulletin*, *123*(2), 123–42.

Borum, R., Cornell, D. G., Modzeleski, W., & Jimerson, S. R. (2010). What can be done about school shootings? A review of the evidence. *Educational Researcher*, *39*(1), 27–37.

Braithwaite, J. (1989). *Crime, shame and reintegration.* Cambridge: Cambridge University Press.

Brank, E. M., Hoetger, L. A., & Hazen, K. P. (2012). Bullying. *Annual Review of Law and Social Science*, *8*, 213–30.

Bronfenbrenner, U. (1979). *The ecology of human development: Experiments by nature and design.* Cambridge, MA: Harvard University Press.

Brown, E. C., Low, S., Smith, B. H., & Haggerty, K. P. (2011). Outcomes from a school-randomized controlled trial of Steps to Respect: A bullying prevention program. *School Psychology Review, 40*(3), 423–43.

Brownson, R. C., Colditz, G. A., & Proctor, E. K. (eds.). (2017). *Dissemination and implementation research in health: Translating science to practice* (second ed.) New York: Oxford University Press.

Bukowski, W. M., Bagwell, C., Castellanos, M., & Persram, R. J. (2020). Friendship in adolescence. In S. Hupp & J. D. Jewell (eds.), *The Encyclopedia of Child and Adolescent Development* (pp. 1–11). Hoboken, NJ: John Wiley & Sons.

Bunch, J., Clay-Warner, J., & McMahon-Howard, J. (2014). The effects of victimization on routine activities. *Criminal Justice and Behavior, 41*(5), 574–92.

Burgess, R. L., & Akers, R. L. (1966). A differential association-reinforcement theory of criminal behavior. *Social Problems, 14*(2), 128–47.

Bushman, B. J., Newman, K., Calvert, S. L., et al. (2016). Youth violence: What we know and what we need to know. *American Psychologist, 71*(1), 17–39.

Camodeca, M., Caravita, S. C., & Coppola, G. (2015). Bullying in preschool: The associations between participant roles, social competence, and social preference. *Aggressive Behavior, 41*(4), 310–21.

Caravita, S. C., di Blasio, P., & Salmivalli, C. (2009). Unique and interactive effects of empathy and social status on involvement in bullying. *Social Development, 18*(1), 140–63.

Carbone-Lopez, K., Esbensen, F. A., & Brick, B. T. (2010). Correlates and consequences of peer victimization: Gender differences in direct and indirect forms of bullying. *Youth Violence and Juvenile Justice, 8*(4), 332–50.

Cecen-Celik, H., & Keith, S. (2019). Analyzing predictors of bullying victimization with routine activity and social bond perspectives. *Journal of Interpersonal Violence, 34*(18), 3807–32.

Chambliss, W. J., & Seidman, R. B. (1971). *Law, order, and power.* Boston: Addison-Wesley.

CHDS K-12 School Shooting Database. (2020). https://www.chds.us/ssdb/ Washington, DC: Center for Homeland Defense and Security.

Chouhy, C., Madero-Hernandez, A., & Turanovic, J. J. (2017). The extent, nature, and consequences of school victimization: A review of surveys and recent research. *Victims & Offenders, 12*(6), 823–44.

Christensen, L. L., Fraynt, R. J., Neece, C. L., & Baker, B. L. (2012). Bullying adolescents with intellectual disability. *Journal of Mental Health Research in Intellectual Disabilities, 5*(1), 49–65.

Chui, W. H., & Chan, H. C. O. (2015). Self-control, school bullying perpetration, and victimization among Macanese adolescents. *Journal of Child and Family Studies, 24*(6), 1751–61.

Cillessen, A. H., & Lansu, T. A. (2015). Stability, correlates, and time-covarying associations of peer victimization from grade 4 to 12. *Journal of Clinical Child & Adolescent Psychology, 44*(3), 456–70.

Cloward, R. A., & Ohlin, L. E. (1960). *Delinquency and opportunity: A theory of delinquent gangs*. New York: The Free Press.

Cohen, A. K. (1955). *Delinquent boys: The culture of the gang*. New York: The Free Press.

Cohen, L. E., & Felson, M. (1979). Social change and crime rate trends: A routine activity approach. *American Sociological Review, 44*(4), 588–608.

Collier, N. L., Brown, S. J., Montes, A. N., Pesta, G. B., Mears, D. P., & Siennick, S. E. (2019). Navigating get-tough and support-oriented philosophies for improving school safety: Insights from school administrators and school safety staff. *American Journal of Criminal Justice, 44*(5), 705–26.

Colvin, M. (2000). *Crime and coercion: An integrated theory of chronic criminality*. New York: St. Martins.

Conduct Problems Prevention Research Group. (1992). A developmental and clinical model for the prevention of conduct disorder: The FAST Track Program. *Development and Psychopathology, 4*(4), 509–27.

Conduct Problems Prevention Research Group. (2011). The effects of the Fast Track preventive intervention on the development of conduct disorder across childhood. *Child Development, 82*(1), 331–45.

Connell, N. M., Morris, R. G., & Piquero, A. R. (2017). Exploring the link between being bullied and adolescent substance use. *Victims & Offenders, 12*(2), 277–96.

Conroy, N. E. (2013). Rethinking adolescent peer sexual harassment: Contributions of feminist theory. *Journal of School Violence, 12*(4), 340–56.

Cook, C. R., Williams, K. R., Guerra, N. G., Kim, T. E., & Sadek, S. (2010). Predictors of bullying and victimization in childhood and adolescence: A meta-analytic investigation. *School Psychology Quarterly, 25*(2), 65–83.

Cook, P. J., Gottfredson, D. C., & Na, C. (2010). School crime control and prevention. *Crime and Justice, 39*(1), 313–440.

Cornell, D. G. (2020). Threat assessment as a school violence prevention strategy. *Criminology & Public Policy, 19*(1), 235–52.

Cosgrove, H. E., & Nickerson, A. B. (2017). Anti-bullying/harassment legislation and educator perceptions of severity, effectiveness, and school climate: A cross-sectional analysis. *Educational Policy, 31*(4), 518–45.

Counts, J., Randall, K. N., Ryan, J. B., & Katsiyannis, A. (2018). School resource officers in public schools: A national review. *Education and Treatment of Children*, *41*(4), 405–30.

Crick, N. R., & Dodge, K. A. (1994). A review and reformulation of social information-processing mechanisms in children's social adjustment. *Psychological Bulletin*, *115*(1), 74–101.

Cullen, D. (2009). *Columbine*. New York: Hachette.

Cullen, F. T. (2005). The twelve people who saved rehabilitation: How the science of criminology made a difference – The American Society of Criminology 2004 presidential address. *Criminology*, *43*(1), 1–42.

Cullen, F. T., Wright, J. P., & Blevins, K. R. (eds.). (2006). *Taking stock: The status of criminological theory – Advances in criminological theory, Vol. 15.* New Brunswick, NJ: Transaction.

Dahlberg, L. L., & Potter, L. B. (2001). Youth violence: Developmental pathways and prevention challenges. *American Journal of Preventive Medicine*, *20*(1), 3–14.

Deakin, J., Taylor, E., & Kupchik, A. (eds.). (2018). *The Palgrave international handbook of school discipline, surveillance, and social control.* London: Palgrave Macmillan.

de Bruyn, E. H., Cillessen, A. H., & Wissink, I. B. (2010). Associations of peer acceptance and perceived popularity with bullying and victimization in early adolescence. *The Journal of Early Adolescence*, *30*(4), 543–66.

DeCamp, W., & Newby, B. (2015). From bullied to deviant: The victim–offender overlap among bullying victims. *Youth Violence and Juvenile Justice*, *13*(1), 3–17.

de Castro, B. O., Veerman, J. W., Koops, W., Bosch, J. D., & Monshouwer, H. J. (2002). Hostile attribution of intent and aggressive behavior: A meta-analysis. *Child Development*, *73*(3), 916–34.

de Ridder, D. T., Lensvelt-Mulders, G., Finkenauer, C., Stok, F. M., & Baumeister, R. F. (2012). Taking stock of self-control: A meta-analysis of how trait self-control relates to a wide range of behaviors. *Personality and Social Psychology Review*, *16*(1), 76–99.

Deryol, R., & Wilcox, P. (2020). Physical health risk factors across traditional bullying and cyberbullying victim and offender groups. *Victims & Offenders*, *15*(4), 520–47.

Deryol, R., Wilcox, P., & Dolu, O. (2017). School-based violent victimization in Turkey: An examination of the cross-national generality of lifestyle-routine activities and self-control theories. *Victims & Offenders*, *12*(6), 913–38.

Destin, M., Richman, S., Varner, F., & Mandara, J. (2012). "Feeling" hierarchy: The pathway from subjective social status to achievement. *Journal of Adolescence, 35*(6), 1571–9.

DeWall, C. N., Twenge, J. M., Gitter, S. A., & Baumeister, R. F. (2009). It's the thought that counts: The role of hostile cognition in shaping aggressive responses to social exclusion. *Journal of Personality and Social Psychology, 96*(1), 45–59.

Dijkstra, J. K., Lindenberg, S., Veenstra, R., et al.et (2010). Influence and selection processes in weapon carrying during adolescence: The roles of status, aggression, and vulnerability. *Criminology, 48*(1), 187–220.

Dodge, K. A., & Coie, J. D. (1987). Social-information-processing factors in reactive and proactive aggression in children's peer groups. *Journal of Personality and Social Psychology, 53*(6), 1146–58.

Dodge, K. A., Greenberg, M. T., Malone, P. S., & The Conduct Problems Prevention Research Group. (2008). Testing an idealized dynamic cascade model of the development of serious violence in adolescence. *Child Development, 79*(6), 1907–27.

Dong, B., Morrison, C. N., Branas, C. C., Richmond, T. S., & Wiebe, D. J. (2020). As violence unfolds: A space-time study of situational triggers of violent victimization among urban youth. *Journal of Quantitative Criminology, 36*(1), 119–52.

Donohue, J. J., & Levitt, S. D. (2001). The impact of legalized abortion on crime. *The Quarterly Journal of Economics, 116*(2), 379–420.

Dooley, B. D. (2021). Establishing a profession through boundary drawing: Defining criminology's autonomy vis-à-vis six competing disciplines. *American Journal of Criminal Justice*, https://doi.org/10.1007/s12103-021-09611-2.

DuRant, R. H., Kahn, J., Beckford, P. H., & Woods, E. R. (1997). The association of weapon carrying and fighting on school property and other health risk and problem behaviors among high school students. *Archives of Pediatrics & Adolescent Medicine, 151*(4), 360–6.

DuRant, R. H., Krowchuk, D. P., Kreiter, S., Sinal, S. H., & Woods, C. R. (1999). Weapon carrying on school property among middle school students. *Archives of Pediatrics & Adolescent Medicine, 153*(1), 21–6.

Duru, E., & Balkis, M. (2018). Exposure to school violence at school and mental health of victimized adolescents: The mediation role of social support. *Child Abuse & Neglect, 76*, 342–52.

Dymnicki, A. B., Weissberg, R. P., & Henry, D. B. (2011). Understanding how programs work to prevent overt aggressive behaviors: A meta-analysis of mediators of elementary school-based programs. *Journal of School Violence*, *10*(4), 315–37.

Egan, S. K., & Perry, D. G. (1998). Does low self-regard invite victimization? *Developmental Psychology*, *34*(2), 299–309.

Eisenberg, M. E., McMorris, B. J., Gower, A. L., & Chatterjee, D. (2016). Bullying victimization and emotional distress: Is there strength in numbers for vulnerable youth? *Journal of Psychosomatic Research*, *86*, 13–19.

Englund, M. M., Levy, A. K., Hyson, D. M., & Sroufe, L. A. (2000). Adolescent social competence: Effectiveness in a group setting. *Child Development*, *71* (4), 1049–60.

Espelage, D. L. (2014). Ecological theory: Preventing youth bullying, aggression, and victimization. *Theory into Practice*, *53*(4), 257–64.

Espelage, D. L., Low, S. K., & Jimerson, S. R. (2014). Understanding school climate, aggression, peer victimization, and bully perpetration: Contemporary science, practice, and policy. *School Psychology Quarterly*, *29*(3), 233–7.

Espelage, D. L., & Swearer, S. M. (2004). *Bullying in American schools: A social-ecological perspective on prevention and intervention*. Mahwah, NJ: Lawrence Erlbaum.

Estévez, E., Murgui, S., & Musitu, G. (2009). Psychological adjustment in bullies and victims of school violence. *European Journal of Psychology of Education*, *24*(4), 473–83.

Faris, R., & Felmlee, D. (2011). Status struggles: Network centrality and gender segregation in same- and cross-gender aggression. *American Sociological Review*, *76*(1), 48–73.

Faris, R., & Felmlee, D. (2014). Casualties of social combat: School networks of peer victimization and their consequences. *American Sociological Review*, *79*(2), 228–57.

Faris, R., Felmlee, D., & McMillan, C. (2020). With friends like these: Aggression from amity and equivalence. *American Journal of Sociology*, *126*(3), 673–713.

Farrington, D. P. (1993). Understanding and preventing bullying. *Crime and Justice*, *17*, 381–458.

Farrington, D. P., Kazemian, L., & Piquero, A. R. (eds.). (2018). *The Oxford handbook of developmental and life-course criminology*. New York: Oxford University Press.

Feldman, A. F., & Matjasko, J. L. (2005). The role of school-based extracurricular activities in adolescent development: A comprehensive review and future directions. *Review of Educational Research*, *75*(2), 159–210.

Felson, M., & Boba, R. (2010). *Crime and everyday life* (fourth ed.). Thousand Oaks, CA: Sage.

Felson, M., & Cohen, L. E. (1980). Human ecology and crime: A routine activity approach. *Human Ecology, 8*(4), 389–406.

Felson, R. B., Berg, M. T., Rogers, E. M., & Krajewski, A. (2018). Disputatiousness and the offender–victim overlap. *Journal of Research in Crime and Delinquency, 55*(3), 351–89.

Felson, R. B., Savolainen, J., Berg, M. T., & Ellonen, N. (2013). Does spending time in public settings contribute to the adolescent risk of violent victimization? *Journal of Quantitative Criminology, 29*(2), 273–93.

Finkelhor, D. (2008). *Childhood victimization: Violence, crime, and abuse in the lives of young people.* New York: Oxford University Press.

Finkelhor, D., & Asdigian, N. L. (1996). Risk factors for youth victimization: Beyond a lifestyles/routine activities theory approach. *Violence and Victims, 11*(1), 3–19.

Finkelhor, D., Vanderminden, J., Turner, H., Shattuck, A., & Hamby, S. (2016). At-school victimization and violence exposure assessed in a national household survey of children and youth. *Journal of School Violence, 15*(1), 67–90.

Fisher, B. W., Nation, M., Nixon, C. T., & McIlroy, S. (2017). Students' perceptions of safety at school after Sandy Hook. *Journal of School Violence, 16*(4), 349–60.

Fite, P. J., Cooley, J. L., & Williford, A. (2020). Components of evidence-based interventions for bullying and peer victimization. In R. G. Steele & M. C. Roberts (eds.), *Handbook of evidence-based therapies for children and adolescents – Issues in clinical child psychology* (pp. 219–234). New York: Springer.

Fite, P. J., Cooley, J. L., Williford, A., Frazer, A., & DiPierro, M. (2014). Parental involvement as a moderator of the association between peer victimization and academic performance. *Children and Youth Services Review, 44,* 25–32.

Forrest, K. Y. Z., Zychowski, A. K., Stuhldreher, W. L., & Ryan, W. J. (2000). Weapon-carrying in school: Prevalence and association with other violent behaviors. *American Journal of Health Studies, 16*(3), 133–40.

Forrest, W., Hay, C., Widdowson, A. O., & Rocque, M. (2019). Development of impulsivity and risk-seeking: Implications for the dimensionality and stability of self-control. *Criminology, 57*(3), 5112–543.

Forsberg, C., & Thornberg, R. (2016). The social ordering of belonging: Children's perspectives on bullying. *International Journal of Educational Research, 78,* 13–23.

Forster, M., Gower, A. L., McMorris, B. J., & Borowsky, I. W. (2020). Adverse childhood experiences and school-based victimization and perpetration. *Journal of Interpersonal Violence, 35*(3–4), 662–81.

Fournier, M. A. (2009). Adolescent hierarchy formation and the social competition theory of depression. *Journal of Social and Clinical Psychology, 28*(9), 1144–72.

Frey, K. S., Hirschstein, M. K., Snell, J. L., Edstrom, L. V. S., MacKenzie, E. P., & Broderick, C. J. (2005). Reducing playground bullying and supporting beliefs: An experimental trial of the steps to respect program. *Developmental Psychology, 41*(3), 479–90.

Fridel, E. E. (2021). The contextual correlates of school shootings. *Justice Quarterly, 38*(4), 596–625.

Gaffney, H., Farrington, D. P., & Ttofi, M. M. (2019). Examining the effectiveness of school-bullying intervention programs globally: A meta-analysis. *International Journal of Bullying Prevention, 1*(1), 14–31.

Gage, N. A., Prykanowski, D. A., & Larson, A. (2014). School climate and bullying victimization: A latent class growth model analysis. *School Psychology Quarterly, 29*(3), 256–71.

Gaias, L. M., Johnson, S. L., White, R. M., Pettigrew, J., & Dumka, L. (2018). Understanding school–neighborhood mesosystemic effects on adolescent development. *Adolescent Research Review, 3*(3), 301–19.

Garandeau, C. F., Lee, I. A., & Salmivalli, C. (2014). Inequality matters: Classroom status hierarchy and adolescents' bullying. *Journal of Youth and Adolescence, 43*(7), 1123–33.

Garbacz, S. A., Watkins, N. D., Diaz, Y., Barnabas Jr, E. R., Schwartz, B., & Eiraldi, R. (2017). Using conjoint behavioral consultation to implement evidence-based practices for students in low-income urban schools. Preventing School Failure: Alternative Education for Children and Youth, 61(3), 198–210.

Garofalo, C., & Velotti, P. (2017). Negative emotionality and aggression in violent offenders: The moderating role of emotion dysregulation. *Journal of Criminal Justice, 51*, 9–16.

Gendreau, P., Little, T., & Goggin, C. (1996). A meta-analysis of the predictors of adult offender recidivism: What works! *Criminology, 34*(4), 575–608.

Georgiou, S. N. (2009). Personal and maternal parameters of peer violence at school. *Journal of School Violence, 8*(2), 100–19.

Gibbs, J. P. (1975). *Crime, punishment, and deterrence.* New York: Elsevier.

Gini, G., Pozzoli, T., & Hymel, S. (2014). Moral disengagement among children and youth: A meta-analytic review of links to aggressive behavior. *Aggressive Behavior, 40*(1), 56–68.

Gleser, L. J., & Olkin, I. (1994). Stochastically dependent effect sizes. In H. Cooper & L. V. Hedges (eds.), *The handbook of research synthesis and meta-analysis* (pp. 339–55). New York: Russell Sage Foundation.

Goldstein, S. E., Young, A., & Boyd, C. (2008). Relational aggression at school: Associations with school safety and social climate. *Journal of Youth and Adolescence, 37*(6), 641–54.

Gottfredson, D. C. (2001). *Schools and delinquency.* Cambridge: Cambridge University Press.

Gottfredson, D. C. (2017). Prevention research in schools: Past, present, and future. Vollmer Award Address. *Criminology & Public Policy, 16*(1), 7–27.

Gottfredson, D. C., & DiPietro, S. M. (2011). School size, social capital, and student victimization. *Sociology of Education, 84*(1), 69–89.

Gottfredson, G. D., Gottfredson, D. C., Czeh, E. R., Cantor, D., Crosse, S., & Hantman, I. (2000). *National study of delinquency prevention in schools.* Ellicott City, MD: Gottfredson Associates. Retrieved from www.ncjrs.gov /pdffiles1/nij/grants/194116.pdf.

Gottfredson, G. D., Gottfredson, D. C., Payne, A. A., & Gottfredson, N. C. (2005). School climate predictors of school disorder: Results from a national study of delinquency prevention in schools. *Journal of Research in Crime and Delinquency, 42*(4), 412–44.

Gottfredson, M. R. (1981). On the etiology of criminal victimization. *Journal of Criminal Law and Criminology, 72*(2), 714–26.

Gottfredson, M. R., & Hirschi, T. (1990). *A general theory of crime.* Stanford, CA: Stanford University Press.

Hanish, L. D., & Guerra, N. G. (2002). A longitudinal analysis of patterns of adjustment following peer victimization. *Development and Psychopathology, 14*(1), 69–89.

Hatchel, T., Ingram, K. M., Mintz, S., et al. (2019). Predictors of suicidal ideation and attempts among LGBTQ adolescents: The roles of help-seeking beliefs, peer victimization, depressive symptoms, and drug use. *Journal of Child and Family Studies, 28*(9), 2443–55.

Hatzenbuehler, M. L., Flores, J. E., Cavanaugh, J. E., Onwuachi-Willig, A., & Ramirez, M. R. (2017). Anti-bullying policies and disparities in bullying: A state-level analysis. *American Journal of Preventive Medicine, 53*(2), 184–91.

Hawkins, J. D., Kosterman, R., Catalano, R. F., Hill, K. G., & Abbott, R. D. (2005). Promoting positive adult functioning through social development intervention in childhood: Long-term effects from the Seattle Social Development Project. *Archives of Pediatrics & Adolescent Medicine, 159*(1), 25–31.

Hawkins, J. D., Smith, B. H., Hill, K. G., Kosterman, R., Catalano, R. F., & Abbott, R. D. (2007). Promoting social development and preventing health and behavior problems during the elementary grades: Results from the Seattle Social Development Project. *Victims & Offenders, 2*(2), 161–81.

Hawley, P. H. (1999). The ontogenesis of social dominance: A strategy-based evolutionary perspective. *Developmental Review, 19*(1), 97–132.

Hedges, L. V., & Olkin, I. (1985). *Statistical methods for meta-analysis.* Orlando, FL: Academic Press.

Hektner, J. M., August, G. J., & Realmuto, G. M. (2000). Patterns and temporal changes in peer affiliation among aggressive and nonaggressive children participating in a summer school program. *Journal of Clinical Child Psychology, 29*(4), 603–14.

Herrenkohl, T. I., Lee, J., & Hawkins, J. D. (2012). Risk versus direct protective factors and youth violence: Seattle Social Development Project. *American Journal of Preventive Medicine, 43*(2), S41–56.

Herrenkohl, T. I., Maguin, E., Hill, K. G., Hawkins, J. D., Abbott, R. D., & Catalano, R. F. (2000). Developmental risk factors for youth violence. *Journal of Adolescent Health, 26*(3), 176–86.

Higgins, G. E., Piquero, N. L., & Piquero, A. R. (2011). General strain theory, peer rejection, and delinquency/crime. *Youth & Society, 43*(4), 1272–97.

Hill, K. G., Howell, J. C., Hawkins, J. D., & Battin-Pearson, S. R. (1999). Childhood risk factors for adolescent gang membership: Results from the Seattle Social Development Project. *Journal of Research in Crime and Delinquency, 36*(3), 300–22.

Hindelang, M. J., Gottfredson, M. R., & Garofalo, J. (1978). *Victims of personal crime: An empirical foundation for a theory of personal victimization.* Cambridge, MA: Ballinger.

Hinduja, S., & Patchin, J. W. (2019). Connecting adolescent suicide to the severity of bullying and cyberbullying. *Journal of School Violence, 18*(3), 333–46.

Hirschfield, P. J. (2008). Preparing for prison? The criminalization of school discipline in the USA. *Theoretical Criminology, 12*(1), 79–101.

Hirschfield, P. J. (2018). Schools and crime. *Annual Review of Criminology, 1*, 149–69.

Hirschi, T. (1969). *Causes of delinquency.* Berkeley: University of California Press.

Hirschi, T., & Gottfredson, M. R. (eds.). (1994). *The generality of deviance.* New Brunswick, NJ: Transaction.

Hoeve, M., Stams, G. J. J., van der Put, C. E., Dubas, J. S., Van der Laan, P. H., & Gerris, J. R. (2012). A meta-analysis of attachment to parents and delinquency. *Journal of Abnormal Child Psychology, 40*(5), 771–85.

Hollis, M. E., Felson, M., & Welsh, B. C. (2013). The capable guardian in routine activities theory: A theoretical and conceptual reappraisal. *Crime Prevention and Community Safety, 15*(1), 65–79.

Homer, E. M., & Fisher, B. W. (2020). Police in schools and student arrest rates across the United States: Examining differences by race, ethnicity, and gender. *Journal of School Violence, 19*(2), 192–204.

Hoover, J. H., Oliver, R., & Hazler, R. J. (1992). Bullying: Perceptions of adolescent victims in the Midwestern USA. *School Psychology International, 13*(1), 5–16.

Hox, J. J. (2010). *Multilevel analysis: Techniques and applications* (second ed.). New York: Routledge.

Huitsing, G., & Monks, C. P. (2018). Who victimizes whom and who defends whom? A multivariate social network analysis of victimization, aggression, and defending in early childhood. *Aggressive Behavior, 44*(4), 394–405.

Huitsing, G., & Veenstra, R. (2012). Bullying in classrooms: Participant roles from a social network perspective. *Aggressive Behavior, 38*(6), 494–509.

Hymel, S., & Swearer, S. M. (2015). Four decades of research on school bullying: An introduction. *American Psychologist, 70*(4), 293–99.

Jacobsen, W. C. (2020). School punishment and interpersonal exclusion: Rejection, withdrawal, and separation from friends. *Criminology, 58*(1), 35–69.

Jambon, M., & Smetana, J. G. (2018). Callous-unemotional traits moderate the association between children's early moral understanding and aggression: A short-term longitudinal study. *Developmental Psychology, 54*(5), 903–95.

James, K., Bunch, J., & Clay-Warner, J. (2015). Perceived injustice and school violence: An application of general strain theory. *Youth Violence and Juvenile Justice, 13*(2), 169–89.

Jeffrey, C. R. (1978). Criminology as an interdisciplinary behavioral science. *Criminology, 16*(2), 149–69.

Jennings, W. G., Khey, D. N., Maskaly, J., & Donner, C. M. (2011). Evaluating the relationship between law enforcement and school security measures and violent crime in schools. *Journal of Police Crisis Negotiations, 11*(2), 109–24.

Jiménez-Barbero, J. A., Jiménez-Loaisa, A., González-Cutre, D., Beltrán-Carrillo, V. J., Llor-Zaragoza, L., & Ruiz-Hernández, J. A. (2020). Physical education and school bullying: A systematic review. *Physical Education and Sport Pedagogy, 25*(1), 79–100.

Jiménez-Barbero, J. A., Ruiz-Hernández, J. A., Llor-Zaragoza, L., Pérez-García, M., & Llor-Esteban, B. (2016). Effectiveness of anti-bullying school programs: A meta-analysis. *Children and Youth Services Review, 61*, 165–75.

Johnson, S. L., Bottiani, J., Waasdorp, T. E., & Bradshaw, C. P. (2018). Surveillance or safekeeping? How school security officer and camera presence influence students' perceptions of safety, equity, and support. *Journal of Adolescent Health*, *63*(6), 732–8.

Jonson, C. L. (2017). Preventing school shootings: The effectiveness of safety measures. *Victims & Offenders*, *12*(6), 956–73.

Jonson, C. L., Moon, M. M., & Hendry, J. A. (2020). One size does not fit all: Traditional lockdown versus multioption responses to school shootings. *Journal of School Violence*, *19*(2), 154–66.

Juvonen, J., & Graham, S. (2001). *Peer harassment in school: The plight of the vulnerable and victimized*. New York: Guilford

Juvonen, J., & Graham, S. (2014). Bullying in schools: The power of bullies and the plight of victims. *Annual Review of Psychology*, *65*, 159–85.

Juvonen, J., & Gross, E. F. (2008). Extending the school grounds? Bullying experiences in cyberspace. *Journal of School Health*, *78*(9), 496–505.

Juvonen, J., Nishina, A., & Graham, S. (2006). Ethnic diversity and perceptions of safety in urban middle schools. *Psychological Science*, *17*(5), 393–400.

Juvonen, J., Schacter, H. L., Sainio, M., & Salmivalli, C. (2016). Can a school-wide bullying prevention program improve the plight of victims? Evidence for risk × intervention effects. *Journal of Consulting and Clinical Psychology*, *84*(4), 334–44.

Kelly, M. B., & McBride, A. B. (2020). *Safe passage: A guide for addressing school violence*. Washington, DC: American Psychiatric Association.

Kempe, C. H., Silverman, F. N., Steele, B. F., Droegemueller, W., & Silver, H. K. (1962). The battered-child syndrome. *Journal of the American Medical Association*, *181*(1), 17–24.

Khanhkham, A., Williams, R. D., Housman, J. M., & Odum, M. (2020). Sexual dating violence, school-based violence, and risky behaviors among U.S. high school students. *Journal of Community Health*, *45*, 932–42.

Kiernan Coon, J. (2021). Situational crime prevention strategies in schools: An assessment of principals' perceptions of the effectiveness of security approaches in public high schools. *Security Journal*, *34*, 635–57.

Killer, B., Bussey, K., Hawes, D. J., & Hunt, C. (2019). A meta-analysis of the relationship between moral disengagement and bullying roles in youth. *Aggressive Behavior*, *45*(4), 450–62.

Kim, B. E., Gilman, A. B., Hill, K. G., & Hawkins, J. D. (2016). Examining protective factors against violence among high-risk youth: Findings from the Seattle Social Development Project. *Journal of Criminal Justice*, *45*, 19–25.

Kokkinos, C. M., & Kipritsi, E. (2012). The relationship between bullying, victimization, trait emotional intelligence, self-efficacy and empathy among preadolescents. *Social Psychology of Education*, *15*(1), 41–58.

Kornienko, O., Dishion, T. J., & Ha, T. (2018). Peer network dynamics and the amplification of antisocial to violent behavior among young adolescents in public middle schools. *Journal of Emotional and Behavioral Disorders*, *26* (1), 21–30.

Kornienko, O., Ha, T., & Dishion, T. J. (2020). Dynamic pathways between rejection and antisocial behavior in peer networks: Update and test of confluence model. *Development and Psychopathology*, *32*(1), 175–88.

Krivo, L. J., & Peterson, R. D. (1996). Extremely disadvantaged neighborhoods and urban crime. *Social Forces*, *75*(2), 619–48.

Kulig, T. C., Cullen, F. T., Wilcox, P., & Chouhy, C. (2019). Personality and adolescent school-based victimization: Do the big five matter? *Journal of School Violence*, *18*(2), 176–99.

Kulig, T. C., Pratt, T. C., Cullen, F. T., Chouhy, C., & Unnever, J. D. (2017). Explaining bullying victimization: Assessing the generality of the low self-control/risky lifestyle model. *Victims & Offenders*, *12*(6), 891–912.

Kupchik, A. (2016). *The real school safety problem: The long-term consequences of harsh school punishment*. Berkeley: University of California Press.

Kupchik, A., & Farina, K. A. (2016). Imitating authority: Students' perceptions of school punishment and security, and bullying victimization. *Youth Violence and Juvenile Justice*, *14*(2), 147–63.

Kusché, C. A. (2020). The PATHS curriculum: Thirty-five years and counting. In D. W. Nagle, C. A. Erdley, & R. A, Schwartz-Mette (eds.), *Social skills across the life span* (pp. 201–19). Cambridge, MA: Academic Press.

Kusché, C. A., & Greenberg, M. T. (1994). *The PATHS curriculum*. Seattle: Developmental Research and Programs.

Ladd, G. W., Ettekal, I., & Kochenderfer-Ladd, B. (2019). Longitudinal changes in victimized youth's social anxiety and solitary behavior. *Journal of Abnormal Child Psychology*, *47*(7), 1211–23.

LaFontana, K. M., & Cillessen, A. H. (2010). Developmental changes in the priority of perceived status in childhood and adolescence. *Social Development*, *19*(1), 130–47.

Lantos, J. D., & Halpern, J. (2015). Bullying, social hierarchies, poverty, and health outcomes. *Pediatrics*, *135*(Supplement 2), S21–3.

Laub, J. H. (2004). The life course of criminology in the United States: The American Society of Criminology 2003 Presidential Address. *Criminology*, *42*(1), 1–26.

Lauritsen, J. L., & Laub, J. H. (2007). Understanding the link between victimization and offending: New reflections on an old idea. *Crime Prevention Studies*, *22*, 55–75.

Lee, D. R., & Cohen, J. W. (2008). Examining strain in a school context. *Youth Violence and Juvenile Justice*, *6*(2), 115–35.

Lee, H., Pickett, J. T., Burton, A. L., Cullen, F. T., Jonson, C. L., & Burton, V. S. (2020). Attributions as anchors: How the public explains school shootings and why it matters. *Justice Quarterly*, https://doi.org/10.1080/07418825 .2020.1769710.

Lee, S., Kim, C. J., & Kim, D. H. (2015). A meta-analysis of the effect of school-based anti-bullying programs. *Journal of Child Health Care*, *19*(2), 136–53.

Legewie, J., & Fagan, J. (2019). Aggressive policing and the educational performance of minority youth. *American Sociological Review*, *84*(2), 220–47.

Lesser, G. S. (1959). The relationships between various forms of aggression and popularity among lower-class children. *Journal of Educational Psychology*, *50*(1), 20–5.

Limber, S. P. (2011). Development, evaluation, and future directions of the Olweus Bullying Prevention Program. *Journal of School Violence*, *10*(1), 71–87.

Lipsey, M. W., & Derzon, J. H. (1998). Predictors of violent or serious delinquency in adolescence and early adulthood: A synthesis of longitudinal research. In R. Loeber & D. P. Farrington (eds.), *Serious & violent juvenile offenders: Risk factors and successful interventions* (pp. 86–105). Thousand Oaks, CA: Sage.

Lipsey, M. W., & Wilson, D. B. (2001). *Practical meta-analysis*. Thousand Oaks, CA: Sage.

Lochman, J. E., & Wells, K. C. (2002). The Coping Power Program at the middle school transition: Universal and indicated prevention effects. *Psychology of Addictive Behaviors*, *16*(4S), S40–54.

Loeber, R., & Le Blanc, M. (1990). Toward a developmental criminology. *Crime and Justice*, *12*, 375–473.

Lonczak, H. S., Abbott, R. D., Hawkins, J. D., Kosterman, R., & Catalano, R. F. (2002). Effects of the Seattle Social Development Project on sexual behavior, pregnancy, birth, and sexually transmitted disease outcomes by age 21 years. *Archives of Pediatrics & Adolescent Medicine*, *156*(5), 438–47.

Low, S., Frey, K. S., & Brockman, C. J. (2010). Gossip on the playground: Changes associated with universal intervention, retaliation beliefs, and supportive friends. *School Psychology Review*, *39*(4), 536–51.

Low, S., van Ryzin, M. J., Brown, E. C., Smith, B. H., & Haggerty, K. P. (2014). Engagement matters: Lessons from assessing classroom implementation of steps to respect: A bullying prevention program over a one-year period. *Prevention Science, 15*(2), 165–76.

Ma, T. L., Meter, D. J., Chen, W. T., & Lee, Y. (2019). Defending behavior of peer victimization in school and cyber context during childhood and adolescence: A meta-analytic review of individual and peer-relational characteristics. *Psychological Bulletin, 145*(9), 891.

Malette, N. (2017). Forms of fighting: A micro-social analysis of bullying and in-school violence. *Canadian Journal of Education, 40*(1), 1–29.

Maynard, B. R., Vaughn, M. G., Salas-Wright, C. P., & Vaughn, S. (2016). Bullying victimization among school-aged immigrant youth in the United States. *Journal of Adolescent Health, 58*(3), 337–44.

Melde, C., & Esbensen, F. A. (2009). The victim–offender overlap and fear of in-school victimization: A longitudinal examination of risk assessment models. *Crime & Delinquency, 55*(4), 499–525.

Menesini, E., & Salmivalli, C. (2017). Bullying in schools: The state of knowledge and effective interventions. *Psychology, Health & Medicine, 22* (Supplement 1), 240–53.

Merrell, K. W., Gueldner, B. A., Ross, S. W., & Isava, D. M. (2008). How effective are school bullying intervention programs? A meta-analysis of intervention research. *School Psychology Quarterly, 23*(1), 26–42.

Merrin, G. J., de la Haye, K., Espelage, D. L., et al. (2018). The co-evolution of bullying perpetration, homophobic teasing, and a school friendship network. *Journal of Youth and Adolescence, 47*(3), 601–18.

Merton, R. K. (1938). Social structure and anomie. *American Sociological Review, 3*(5), 672–82.

Metzler, M., Merrick, M. T., Klevens, J., Ports, K. A., & Ford, D. C. (2017). Adverse childhood experiences and life opportunities: Shifting the narrative. *Children and Youth Services Review, 72*, 141–9.

Meyer-Adams, N., & Conner, B. T. (2008). School violence: Bullying behaviors and the psychosocial school environment in middle schools. *Children & Schools, 30*(4), 211–21.

Moeyaert, M., Ugille, M., Natasha Beretvas, S., Ferron, J., Bunuan, R., & van den Noortgate, W. (2017). Methods for dealing with multiple outcomes in meta-analysis: A comparison between averaging effect sizes, robust variance estimation and multilevel meta-analysis. *International Journal of Social Research Methodology, 20*(6), 559–72.

Moher, D., Liberati, A., Tetzlaff, J., Altman, D. G., & Prisma Group. (2009). Preferred reporting items for systematic reviews and meta-analyses: The PRISMA statement. *PLoS Medicine, 6*(7), e1000097.

Moon, B., & Alarid, L. F. (2015). School bullying, low self-control, and opportunity. *Journal of Interpersonal Violence, 30*(5), 839–56.

Mouttapa, M., Valente, T., Gallaher, P., Rohrbach, L. A., & Unger, J. B. (2004). Social network predictors of bullying and victimization. *Adolescence, 39* (154), 315–35.

Mowen, T., & Brent, J. (2016). School discipline as a turning point: The cumulative effect of suspension on arrest. *Journal of Research in Crime and Delinquency, 53*(5), 628–53.

Mowen, T. J., & Freng, A. (2019). Is more necessarily better? School security and perceptions of safety among students and parents in the United States. *American Journal of Criminal Justice, 44*(3), 376–94.

Mulvey, K. L., Boswell, C., & Zheng, J. (2017). Causes and consequences of social exclusion and peer rejection among children and adolescents. *Report on Emotional & Behavioral Disorders in Youth, 17*(3), 71–5.

Myers, W., Turanovic, J. J., Lloyd, K. M., & Pratt, T. C. (2020). The victimization of LGBTQ students at school: A meta-analysis. *Journal of School Violence, 19*(4), 421–32.

Na, C., & Gottfredson, D. C. (2013). Police officers in schools: Effects on school crime and the processing of offending behaviors. *Justice Quarterly, 30* (4), 619–50.

Nail, P. R., Simon, J. B., Bihm, E. M., & Beasley, W. H. (2016). Defensive egotism and bullying: Gender differences yield qualified support for the compensation model of aggression. *Journal of School Violence, 15*(1), 22–47.

National School Climate Council. (2007). *The school climate challenge: Narrowing the gap between school climate research and school climate policy, practice guide-lines and teacher education policy.* Retrieved from www.schoolclimate.org/climate/advocacy.php.

Niemi, R. G. (1986). Series editor's introduction. In F. M. Wolf (ed.), *Meta-analysis: Quantitative methods for research synthesis* (pp. 5–6). Newbury Park, CA: Sage.

Nocentini, A., & Menesini, E. (2016). KiVa anti-bullying program in Italy: Evidence of effectiveness in a randomized control trial. *Prevention Science, 17*(8), 1012–23.

Olweus, D. (1977). Aggression and peer acceptance in adolescent boys: Two short-term longitudinal studies. *Child Development, 48*(4), 1301–13.

Olweus, D. (1978). *Aggression in the schools: Bullies and whipping boys.* Washington, DC: Hemisphere.

Olweus, D. (2013). School bullying: Development and some important challenges. *Annual Review of Clinical Psychology, 9*, 751–80.

Olweus, D., & Limber, S. P. (2010). Bullying in school: Evaluation and dissemination of the Olweus Bullying Prevention Program. *American Journal of Orthopsychiatry, 80*(1), 124–34.

Osgood, D. W., Anderson, A. L., & Shaffer, J. N. (2005). Unstructured leisure in the after-school hours. In J. L. Mahoney, R. W. Larson, & J. S. Eccles (eds.), *Organized activities as contexts of development: Extracurricular activities, after-school and community programs* (pp. 45–64). Mahwah, NJ: Lawrence Erlbaum.

Ousey, G. C., & Kubrin, C. E. (2018). Immigration and crime: Assessing a contentious issue. *Annual Review of Criminology, 1*, 63–84.

Ousey, G. C., & Wilcox, P. (2005). Subcultural values and violent delinquency: A multilevel analysis in middle schools. *Youth Violence and Juvenile Justice, 3*(1), 3–22.

Ousey, G. C., Wilcox, P., & Brummel, S. (2008). Déjà vu all over again: Investigating temporal continuity of adolescent victimization. *Journal of Quantitative Criminology, 24*(3), 307–35.

Park, H. S. (2008). Centering in hierarchical linear modeling. *Communication Methods and Measures, 2*(4), 227–59.

Paternoster, R. (1987). The deterrent effect of the perceived certainty and severity of punishment: A review of the evidence and issues. *Justice Quarterly, 4*(2), 173–217.

Patterson, G. R. (1986). Performance models for antisocial boys. *American Psychologist, 41*(4), 432–44.

Peguero, A. A. (2008a). Bullying victimization and extracurricular activity. *Journal of School Violence, 7*(3), 71–85.

Peguero, A. A. (2008b). Is immigrant status relevant in school violence research? An analysis with Latino students. *Journal of School Health, 78*(7), 397–404.

Peguero, A. A. (2013). An adolescent victimization immigrant paradox? School-based routines, lifestyles, and victimization across immigration generations. *Journal of Youth and Adolescence, 42*(11), 1759–73.

Peguero, A. A., & Jiang, X. (2014). Social control across immigrant generations: Adolescent violence at school and examining the immigrant paradox. *Journal of Criminal Justice, 42*(3), 276–87.

Peguero, A. A., & Jiang, X. (2016). Backlash for breaking racial and ethnic breaking stereotypes: Adolescent school victimization across contexts. *Journal of Interpersonal Violence, 31*(6), 1047–73.

Pellegrini, A. D., & Long, J. D. (2002). A longitudinal study of bullying, dominance, and victimization during the transition from primary school through secondary school. *British Journal of Developmental Psychology*, *20*(2), 259–80.

Polanin, J. R., Espelage, D. L., Grotpeter, J. K., et al. (2021). A meta-analysis of longitudinal partial correlations between school violence and mental health, school performance, and criminal or delinquent acts. *Psychological Bulletin*, *147*(2), 115–33.

Popp, A. M., & Peguero, A. A. (2011). Routine activities and victimization at school: The significance of gender. *Journal of Interpersonal Violence, 26* (12), 2413–36.

Postigo, S., González, R., Mateu, C., & Montoya, I. (2012). Predicting bullying: Maladjustment, social skills and popularity. *Educational Psychology*, *32*(5), 627–39.

Pouwels, J. L., Lansu, T. A., & Cillessen, A. H. (2018). A developmental perspective on popularity and the group process of bullying. *Aggression and Violent Behavior*, *43*, 64–70.

Pratt, T. C. (2010). Meta-analysis in criminal justice and criminology: What it is, when it's useful, and what to watch out for. *Journal of Criminal Justice Education*, *21*, 152–68.

Pratt, T. C., & Cullen, F. T. (2000). The empirical status of Gottfredson and Hirschi's general theory of crime: A meta-analysis. *Criminology*, *38*(3), 931–64.

Pratt, T. C., & Cullen, F. T. (2005). Assessing macro-level predictors and theories of crime: A meta-analysis. *Crime and Justice*, *32*, 373–450.

Pratt, T. C., Cullen, F. T., Blevins, K. R., Daigle, L. E., & Madensen, T. D. (2006). The empirical status of deterrence theory: A meta-analysis. In F. T. Cullen, J. P. Wright, & K. R. Blevins (eds.), *Taking stock: The status of criminological theory – Advances in criminological theory, Vol. 15* (pp. 367–95). New Brunswick, NJ: Transaction.

Pratt, T. C., Cullen, F. T., Sellers, C. S., et al. (2010). The empirical status of social learning theory: A meta-analysis. *Justice Quarterly*, *27*(6), 765–802.

Pratt, T. C., & Turanovic, J. J. (2016). Lifestyle and routine activity theories revisited: The importance of "risk" to the study of victimization. *Victims & Offenders*, *11*(3), 335–54.

Pratt, T. C., & Turanovic, J. J. (2018). Celerity and deterrence. In D. S. Nagin, F. T. Cullen, & C. L. Jonson (eds.), *Deterrence, choice, and crime: Contemporary perspectives – Advances in criminological theory, Vol. 23* (pp. 187–210). New York: Routledge.

Pratt, T. C., Turanovic, J. J., Fox, K. A., & Wright, K. A. (2014). Self-control and victimization: A meta-analysis. *Criminology*, *52*(1), 87–116.

Proctor, E. K., Landsverk, J., Aarons, G., Chambers, D., Glisson, C., & Mittman, B. (2009). Implementation research in mental health services: An emerging science with conceptual, methodological, and training challenges. *Administration and Policy in Mental Health, 36*(1), 24–34.

Pyrooz, D. C., Turanovic, J. J., Decker, S. H., & Wu, J. (2016). Taking stock of the relationship between gang membership and offending: A meta-analysis. *Criminal Justice and Behavior, 43*(3), 365–97.

Rambaran, J. A., Dijkstra, J. K., & Veenstra, R. (2020). Bullying as a group process in childhood: A longitudinal social network analysis. *Child Development, 91*(4), 1336–52.

Randa, R., Reyns, B. W., & Nobles, M. R. (2019). Measuring the effects of limited and persistent school bullying victimization: Repeat victimization, fear, and adaptive behaviors. *Journal of Interpersonal Violence, 34*(2), 392–415.

Randa, R., & Wilcox, P. (2012). Avoidance at school: Further specifying the influence of disorder, victimization, and fear. *Youth Violence and Juvenile Justice, 10*(2), 190–204.

Raudenbush, S. W., & Bryk, A. (2002). *Hierarchical linear models: Applications and data analysis methods*. Thousand Oaks, CA: Sage.

Reid, J. A., & Sullivan, C. J. (2009). A latent class typology of juvenile victims and exploration of risk factors and outcomes of victimization. *Criminal Justice and Behavior, 36*(10), 1001–24.

Renzetti, C. M. (2013). *Feminist criminology*. Abingdon: Routledge.

Riese, A., Gjelsvik, A., & Ranney, M. L. (2015). Extracurricular activities and bullying perpetration: Results from a nationally representative sample. *Journal of School Health, 85*(8), 544–51.

Rinehart, S. J., & Espelage, D. L. (2016). A multilevel analysis of school climate, homophobic name-calling, and sexual harassment victimization/perpetration among middle school youth. *Psychology of Violence, 6*(2), 213–22.

Ringwalt, C., Hanley, S., Ennett, S. T., et al. (2011). The effects of No Child Left Behind on the prevalence of evidence-based drug prevention curricula in the nation's middle schools. *Journal of School Health, 81*(5), 265–72.

Rodkin, P. C., Espelage, D. L., & Hanish, L. D. (2015). A relational framework for understanding bullying: Developmental antecedents and outcomes. *American Psychologist, 70*(4), 311–21.

Rodkin, P. C., Farmer, T. W., Pearl, R., & Acker, R. V. (2006). They're cool: Social status and peer group supports for aggressive boys and girls. *Social Development, 15*(2), 175–204.

Roos, L. L., Wall-Wieler, E., & Lee, J. B. (2019). Poverty and early childhood outcomes. *Pediatrics, 143*(6), e20183426.

Rose, I. (2018). *School violence: Studies in alienation, revenge and redemption.* New York: Routledge.

Rose-Krasnor, L. (1997). The nature of social competence: A theoretical review. *Social Development, 6*(1), 111–35.

Rosenthal, R., & Rubin, D. B. (1986). Meta-analytic procedures for combining studies with multiple effect sizes. *Psychological Bulletin, 99*(3), 400–6.

Saarento, S., Kärnä, A., Hodges, E. V., & Salmivalli, C. (2013). Student-, classroom-, and school-level risk factors for victimization. *Journal of School Psychology, 51*(3), 421–34.

Sailor, W., Skrtic, T. M., Cohn, M., & Olmstead, C. (2021). Preparing teacher educators for statewide scale-up of Multi-Tiered System of Support (MTSS). *Teacher Education and Special Education, 44*(1), 24–41.

Salmivalli, C. (2010). Bullying and the peer group: A review. *Aggression and Violent Behavior, 15*, 112–20.

Salmivalli, C., Kärnä, A., & Poskiparta, E. (2011). Counteracting bullying in Finland: The KiVa program and its effects on different forms of being bullied. *International Journal of Behavioral Development, 35*(5), 405–11.

Sampson, R. J. (2012). *Great American city: Chicago and the enduring neighborhood effect.* Chicago: University of Chicago Press.

Savage, J. (2014). The association between attachment, parental bonds and physically aggressive and violent behavior: A comprehensive review. *Aggression and Violent Behavior, 19*(2), 164–78.

Scheckner, S., Rollin, S. A., Kaiser-Ulrey, C., & Wagner, R. (2002). School violence in children and adolescents: A meta-analysis of the effectiveness of current interventions. *Journal of School Violence, 1*(2), 5–32.

Schildkraut, J., & Grogan, K. (2019). *Are metal detectors effective at making schools safer?* San Francisco: WestEd.

Schildkraut, J., & Nickerson, A. B. (2020). Ready to respond: Effects of lockdown drills and training on school emergency preparedness. *Victims & Offenders, 15*(5), 619–38.

Schott, R. M., & Søndergaard, D. M. (eds.). (2014). *School bullying: New theories in context.* New York: Cambridge University Press.

Schreck, C. J. (1999). Criminal victimization and low self-control: An extension and test of a general theory of crime. *Justice Quarterly, 16*(3), 633–54.

Schreck, C. J., Miller, J. M., & Gibson, C. L. (2003). Trouble in the school yard: A study of the risk factors of victimization at school. *Crime & Delinquency, 49*(3), 460–84.

Schreck, C. J., Wright, R. A., & Miller, J. M. (2002). A study of individual and situational antecedents of violent victimization. *Justice Quarterly, 19*(1), 159–80.

Sharkey, P. (2010). The acute effect of local homicides on children's cognitive performance. *Proceedings of the National Academy of Sciences, 107*(26), 11733–8.

Sharkey, P. (2018). The long reach of violence: A broader perspective on data, theory, and evidence on the prevalence and consequences of exposure to violence. *Annual Review of Criminology, 1*, 85–102.

Shaw, C. R., & McKay, H. D. (1942). *Juvenile delinquency and urban areas*. Chicago: University of Chicago Press.

Sidanius, J., & Pratto, F. (1999). *Social dominance: An intergroup theory of social hierarchy and oppression*. New York: Cambridge University Press.

Siddaway, A. P., Wood, A. M., & Hedges, L. V. (2019). How to do a systematic review: A best practice guide for conducting and reporting narrative reviews, meta-analyses, and meta-syntheses. *Annual Review of Psychology, 70*, 747–70.

Sijtsema, J. J., Lindenberg, S. M., & Veenstra, R. (2010). Do they get what they want or are they stuck with what they can get? Testing homophily against default selection for friendships of highly aggressive boys. The TRAILS study. *Journal of Abnormal Child Psychology, 38*(6), 803–13.

Sijtsema, J. J., Veenstra, R., Lindenberg, S., & Salmivalli, C. (2009). Empirical test of bullies' status goals: Assessing direct goals, aggression, and prestige. *Aggressive Behavior, 35*(1), 57–67.

Slaughter, V., Imuta, K., Peterson, C. C., & Henry, J. D. (2015). Meta-analysis of theory of mind and peer popularity in the preschool and early school years. *Child Development, 86*(4), 1159–74.

Son, E., Parish, S. L., & Peterson, N. A. (2012). National prevalence of peer victimization among young children with disabilities in the United States. *Children and Youth Services Review, 34*(8), 1540–5.

Song, J., & Oh, I. (2017). Investigation of the bystander effect in school bullying: Comparison of experiential, psychological and situational factors. *School Psychology International, 38*(3), 319–36.

South, S. J., & Deane, G. D. (1993). Race and residential mobility: Individual determinants and structural constraints. *Social Forces, 72*(1), 147–67.

Spoth, R., Rohrbach, L. A., Greenberg, M., et al. (2013). Addressing core challenges for the next generation of type 2 translation research and systems: The translation science to population impact (TSci Impact) framework. *Prevention Science, 14*(4), 319–51.

Steffgen, G., Recchia, S., & Viechtbauer, W. (2013). The link between school climate and violence in school: A meta-analytic review. *Aggression and Violent Behavior, 18*(2), 300–9.

Stevens, G. W., Boer, M., Titzmann, P. F., Cosma, A., & Walsh, S. D. (2020). Immigration status and bullying victimization: Associations across national and school contexts. *Journal of Applied Developmental Psychology, 66,* 101075.

Sullivan, T. N., Farrell, A. D., & Kliewer, W. (2006). Peer victimization in early adolescence: Association between physical and relational victimization and drug use, aggression, and delinquent behaviors among urban middle school students. *Development and Psychopathology, 18*(1), 119–37.

Sutherland, E. H. (1924). *Criminology.* Philadelphia: J. B. Lippincott.

Swartz, K., Wilcox, P., & Ousey, G. C. (2017). Culture as values or culture in action? Street codes and student violent offending. *Victims & Offenders, 12* (6), 868–90.

Swearer, S. M., & Espelage, D. L. (2011). Expanding the social-ecological framework of bullying among youth: Lessons learned from the past and directions for the future. In D. L. Espelage & S. M. Swearer (eds.), *Bullying in North American schools* (pp. 3–10). New York: Routledge

Swearer, S. M., & Hymel, S. (2015). Understanding the psychology of bullying: Moving toward a social-ecological diathesis–stress model. *American Psychologist, 70*(4), 344–53.

Swearer, S. M., Wang, C., Berry, B., & Myers, Z. R. (2014). Reducing bullying: Application of social cognitive theory. *Theory Into Practice, 53*(4), 271–7.

Tanner, J., Asbridge, M., & Wortley, S. (2015). Leisure worlds: Situations, motivations and young people's encounters with offending and victimization. *Youth & Society, 47*(2), 199–221.

Tanner-Smith, E. E., & Fisher, B. W. (2016). Visible school security measures and student academic performance, attendance, and postsecondary aspirations. *Journal of Youth and Adolescence, 45*(1), 195–210.

Tanner-Smith, E. E., Fisher, B. W., Addington, L. A., & Gardella, J. H. (2018). Adding security, but subtracting safety? Exploring schools' use of multiple visible security measures. *American Journal of Criminal Justice, 43*(1), 102–19.

Thoits, P. A. (2011). Mechanisms linking social ties and support to physical and mental health. *Journal of Health and Social Behavior, 52*(2), 145–61.

Thomas, H. J., Connor, J. P., & Scott, J. G. (2018). Why do children and adolescents bully their peers? A critical review of key theoretical frameworks. *Social Psychiatry and Psychiatric Epidemiology, 53*(5), 437–51.

Tibbits, M. K., Bumbarger, B. K., Kyler, S. J., & Perkins, D. F. (2010). Sustaining evidence-based interventions under real-world conditions: Results from a large-scale diffusion project. *Prevention Science, 11*(3), 252–62.

Tillyer, M. S., Wilcox, P., & Fissel, E. R. (2018). Violence in schools: Repeat victimization, low self-control, and the mitigating influence of school efficacy. *Journal of Quantitative Criminology*, *34*(2), 609–32.

Tippett, N., & Wolke, D. (2014). Socioeconomic status and bullying: A meta-analysis. *American Journal of Public Health*, *104*(6), e48–59.

Tremblay, R. E., & Craig, W. M. (1995). Developmental crime prevention. *Crime and Justice*, *17*, 151–236.

Troop-Gordon, W. (2017). Peer victimization in adolescence: The nature, progression, and consequences of being bullied within a developmental context. *Journal of Adolescence*, *55*, 116–28.

Ttofi, M. M., & Farrington, D. P. (2011). Effectiveness of school-based programs to reduce bullying: A systematic and meta-analytic review. *Journal of Experimental Criminology*, *7*(1), 27–56.

Turanovic, J. J., & Pratt, T. C. (2014). "Can't stop, won't stop": Self-control, risky lifestyles, and repeat victimization. *Journal of Quantitative Criminology*, *30*(1), 29–56.

Turanovic, J. J., & Pratt, T. C. (2015). Longitudinal effects of violent victimization during adolescence on adverse outcomes in adulthood: A focus on prosocial attachments. *Journal of Pediatrics*, *166*(4), 1062–9.

Turanovic, J. J., & Pratt, T. C. (2019). *Thinking about victimization: Context and consequences*. London: Routledge.

Turanovic, J. J., & Pratt, T. C. (2021). Meta-analysis in criminology and criminal justice: Challenging the paradigm and charting a new path forward. *Justice Evaluation Journal*, *4*(1), 21–47.

Turanovic, J. J., Reisig, M. D., & Pratt, T. C. (2015). Risky lifestyles, low self-control, and violent victimization across gendered pathways to crime. *Journal of Quantitative Criminology*, *31*(2), 183–206.

Turanovic, J. J., & Young, J. T. N. (2016). Violent offending and victimization in adolescence: Social network mechanisms and homophily. *Criminology*, *54* (3), 487–519.

Twyman, K. A., Saylor, C. F., Saia, D., Macias, M. M., Taylor, L. A., & Spratt, E. (2010). Bullying and ostracism experiences in children with special health care needs. *Journal of Developmental & Behavioral Pediatrics*, *31*(1), 1–8.

Unnever, J. D., & Cornell, D. G. (2003). Bullying, self-control, and ADHD. *Journal of Interpersonal Violence*, *18*(2), 129–47.

Unnever, J. D., & Gabbidon, S. L. (2011). *A theory of African American offending: Race, racism, and crime*. New York: Routledge.

van den Noortgate, W., López-López, J. A., Marín-Martínez, F., & Sánchez-Meca, J. (2013). Three-level meta-analysis of dependent effect sizes. *Behavior Research Methods*, *45*(2), 576–94.

van der Ploeg, R., Steglich, C., & Veenstra, R. (2020). The way bullying works: How new ties facilitate the mutual reinforcement of status and bullying in elementary schools. *Social Networks, 60*, 71–82.

Varela, J. J., Sirlopú, D., Melipillán, R., Espelage, D., Green, J., & Guzmán, J. (2019). Exploring the influence school climate on the relationship between school violence and adolescent subjective well-being. *Child Indicators Research, 12*(6), 2095–110.

Veenstra, R., Lindenberg, S., Oldehinkel, A. J., de Winter, A. F., Verhulst, F. C., & Ormel, J. (2005). Bullying and victimization in elementary schools: A comparison of bullies, victims, bully/victims, and uninvolved preadolescents. *Developmental Psychology, 41*(4), 672–82.

Veenstra, R., Lindenberg, S., Zijlstra, B. J. H., de Winter, A. F., Verhulst, F. C., & Ormel, J. (2007). The dyadic nature of bullying and victimization: Testing a dual-perspective theory. *Child Development, 78* (6), 1843–54.

Viano, S., Curran, F. C., & Fisher, B. W. (2021). Kindergarten cop: A case study of how a coalition between school districts and law enforcement led to school resource officers in elementary schools. *Educational Evaluation and Policy Analysis, 43*(2), 253–79.

Vitoroulis, I., & Georgiades, K. (2017). Bullying among immigrant and non-immigrant early adolescents: School-and student-level effects. *Journal of Adolescence, 61*, 141–51.

Walsh, A., & Ellis, L. (2007). *Criminology: An interdisciplinary approach.* Thousand Oaks, CA: Sage.

Walters, G. D. (2018). Starting off on the wrong foot: Cognitive impulsivity and low self-control as predictors of early school maladjustment. *Deviant Behavior, 39*(10), 1322–35.

Wang, K., Chen, Y., Zhang, J., & Oudekerk, B. A. (2020). *Indicators of school crime and safety: 2019.* Washington, DC: National Center for Education Statistics, US Department of Education, and Bureau of Justice Statistics, Office of Justice Programs, US Department of Justice.

Wanless, S. B., & Domitrovich, C. E. (2015). Readiness to implement school-based social-emotional learning interventions: Using research on factors related to implementation to maximize quality. *Prevention Science, 16*(8), 1037–43.

Wei, H. S., Williams, J. H., Chen, J. K., & Chang, H. Y. (2010). The effects of individual characteristics, teacher practice, and school organizational factors on students' bullying: A multilevel analysis of public middle schools in Taiwan. *Children and Youth Services Review, 32*(1), 137–43.

Weisburd, D., Farrington, D. P., & Gill, C. (eds.). (2016). *What works in crime prevention and rehabilitation: Lessons from systematic reviews.* New York: Springer.

Welch, K., & Payne, A. A. (2010). Racial threat and punitive school discipline. *Social Problems, 57*(1), 25–48.

Welch, K., & Payne, A. A. (2018). Zero tolerance school policies. In J. Deacon, E. Taylor, & A. Kupchik (eds.), *The Palgrave international handbook of school discipline, surveillance, and social control* (pp. 215–34). London: Palgrave Macmillan.

Welsh, W. N. (2001). Effects of student and school factors on five measures of school disorder. *Justice Quarterly, 18*(4), 911–47.

West, D. J., & Farrington, D. P. (1973). *Who becomes delinquent? Second report of the Cambridge Study in Delinquent Development.* London: Heinmann.

Wilcox, P., Augustine, M. C., & Clayton, R. R. (2006). Physical environment and crime and misconduct in Kentucky schools. *Journal of Primary Prevention, 27*(3), 293–313.

Wilcox, P., & Clayton, R. R. (2001). A multilevel analysis of school-based weapon possession. *Justice Quarterly, 18*(3), 509–41.

Wilcox, P., & Cullen, F. T. (2018). Situational opportunity theories of crime. *Annual Review of Criminology, 1*, 123–48.

Wilcox, P., May, D. C., & Roberts, S. D. (2006). Student weapon possession and the "fear and victimization hypothesis": Unraveling the temporal order. *Justice Quarterly, 23*(4), 502–29.

Wilcox, P., Tillyer, M. S., & Fisher, B. S. (2009). Gendered opportunity? School-based adolescent victimization. *Journal of Research in Crime and Delinquency, 46*(2), 245–69.

Wilcox Rountree, P. (2000). Weapons at school: Are the predictors generalizable across context? *Sociological Spectrum, 20*(3), 291–324.

Wilcox Rountree, P., Land, K. C., & Miethe, T. D. (1994). Macro-micro integration in the study of victimization: A hierarchical logistic model analysis across Seattle neighborhoods. *Criminology, 32*(3), 387–414.

Wiley, S. A., Slocum, L. A., O'Neill, J., & Esbensen, F. A. (2020). Beyond the Breakfast Club: Variability in the effects of suspensions by school context. *Youth & Society, 52*(7), 1259–84.

Williford, A., Boulton, A., Noland, B., Little, T. D., Kärnä, A., & Salmivalli, C. (2012). Effects of the KiVa anti-bullying program on adolescents' depression, anxiety, and perception of peers. *Journal of Abnormal Child Psychology, 40*(2), 289–300.

Wilson, J. Q., & Herrnstein, R. J. (1985). *Crime and human nature.* New York: The Free Press.

Wolfe, S. E., & Lawson, S. G. (2020). The organizational justice effect among criminal justice employees: A meta-analysis. *Criminology, 58*(4), 619–44.

Woolf, S. H. (2008). The meaning of translation research and why it matters. *Journal of the American Medical Association, 299*(2), 211–13.

Wright, J. C., Giammarino, M., & Parad, H. W. (1986). Social status in small groups: Individual-group similarity and the social "misfit." *Journal of Personality and Social Psychology, 50*(3), 523–36.

Wright, K. A., Turanovic, J. J., O'Neal, E. N., Morse, S. J., & Booth, E. T. (2019). The cycle of violence revisited: Childhood victimization, resilience, and future violence. *Journal of Interpersonal Violence, 34*(6), 1261–86.

Ybarra, M. L., Espelage, D. L., & Mitchell, K. J. (2014). Differentiating youth who are bullied from other victims of peer-aggression: The importance of differential power and repetition. *Journal of Adolescent Health, 55*(2), 293–300.

Young, J. (1999). *The exclusive society: Social exclusion, crime and difference in late modernity.* Thousand Oaks, CA: Sage.

Zalba, S. R. (1966). The abused child: I. A survey of the problem. *Social Work, 11*(4), 3–16.

Zaykowski, H., & Gunter, W. (2012). Youth victimization: School climate or deviant lifestyles? *Journal of Interpersonal Violence, 27*(3), 431–52.

Zimmer-Gembeck, M. (2016). Peer rejection, victimization, and relational self-system processes in adolescence: Toward a transactional model of stress, coping, and developing sensitivities. *Child Development Perspectives, 10*(2), 122–7.

Zych, I., Ttofi, M. M., & Farrington, D. P. (2019). Empathy and callous-unemotional traits in different bullying roles: A systematic review and meta-analysis. *Trauma, Violence, & Abuse, 20*(1), 3–21.

Acknowledgments

We are thankful to Meghan Ogle, Wesley Myers, Julie Kuper, and Kristin Lloyd for their assistance with various aspects of this project. This research was supported by Award No. 2015-CK-BX-0001, awarded by the National Institute of Justice, Office of Justice Programs, U.S. Department of Justice, under the Comprehensive School Safety Initiative. The opinions, findings, conclusions, and recommendations expressed in this publication are those of the authors and do not necessarily reflect those of the Department of Justice. Data and supplemental files for this research are available on the Open Science Framework (https://osf.io/7jhy6/).

Cambridge Elements ⁼

Criminology

David Weisburd
George Mason University, Virginia
Hebrew University of Jerusalem

Advisory Board

Professor Catrien Bijleveld, *VU University Amsterdam*
Professor Francis Cullen, *University of Cincinnati*
Professor Manuel Eisner, *Cambridge University*
Professor Elizabeth Groff, *Temple University*
Professor Cynthia Lum, *George Mason University*
Professor Lorraine Mazerolle, *University of Queensland*
Professor Daniel Nagin, *Carnegie Mellon University*
Professor Ojmarrh Mitchell, *Arizona State University*
Professor Alex Piquero, *University of Miami*
Professor Richard Rosenfeld, *University of Missouri St. Louis*

About the Series

Elements in Criminology seeks to identify key contributions in theory and empirical research that help to identify, enable, and stake out advances in contemporary criminology. The series will focus on radical new ways of understanding and framing criminology, whether of place, communities, persons, or situations. The relevance of criminology for preventing and controlling crime will also be a key focus of this series.

Cambridge Elements ^Ξ

Criminology

Elements in the series

Printed in the United States
by Baker & Taylor Publisher Services